Department of Health

Report on Health and Social Subject

37

Dietary Sugars and Human Disease

Report of the Panel on
Dietary Sugars

Committee on Medical Aspects
of Food Policy

London: HMSO

© Crown copyright 1989
First published 1989
Second impression 1991

ISBN 0 11 321255 0

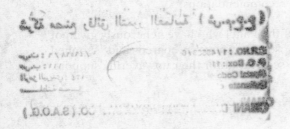

OMANI DATES FLAKE FACTORY CO. (S.A.O.G.)

C.R.NO.:1/405537/6
P.O. Box: 771
Postal Code 124
Sultanate of Oman

Preface

In June 1986 the Committee on Medical Aspects of Food Policy convened a Panel to inquire into and report on the health aspects of the consumption of sugars in United Kingdom diets.

The Panel met on ten occasions and reviewed much published information. It invited and received written submissions from a variety of interested organisations and individuals. This report summarises the findings of the Panel and gives its conclusions and recommendations.

I am very grateful to the members of the Panel who have generously given of their time and knowledge, to those who have prepared and supplied information for the Panel and to the secretariat for their unwavering support.

SIR DONALD ACHESON
Chairman of Committee on Medical Aspects of Food Policy

Committee on Medical Aspects of Food Policy

Panel on Dietary Sugars*

Members

H Keen (Chairman)

A Black
J Durnin
J Garrow
K Heaton
A Jackson

J Mann
D Naismith
E Newsholme
N Read
A Rugg-Gunn
T Silverstone

Observers

J Ablett
D Buss

P Clarke
C Howard

Secretariat

M Wiseman
(Medical)

R Wenlock
(Scientific)

K Follin
(Administrative)

N Bateson (Minutes)
E Lohani (Minutes)
D Roberts (Minutes)

For title and affiliation see Appendix A, page 86

Contents

1. Introduction

1.1 Background to the Panel

1.1.1 In its Report published in 1984[1] the Panel on Diet in relation to Cardiovascular Disease of the Committee on Medical Aspects of Food Policy (COMA) recommended to the general public that 'intake of simple sugars (sucrose, glucose and fructose) should not be increased further', and that 'these sugars and foods containing them are appreciable sources of food energy and may contribute to obesity. Certain foods containing these sugars may also contain saturated fatty acids (eg cakes and biscuits)'. It also noted that 'restriction of intake of these sugars has been recommended on other health grounds (eg dental caries)'.

1.1.2 COMA has noted the conflicting evidence and changing opinion in recent years about the role of dietary sugars in cardiovascular disease, dental caries and other disorders. It has considered the views expressed in two recent exert reports on sugars in the diet, one in the UK[2] and the other from the United States.[3] In 1986 COMA convened this Panel on Dietary Sugars to review the role of dietary sugars in disease in the United Kingdom.

1.2 Terms of reference of the Panel

'To examine the role of dietary sugars in human disease and to make recommendations'.

1.3 Interpretation of terms of reference

Although the Panel has concerned itself with carbohydrate foods with the chemical characteristics of sugars, it has given particular attention to sucrose as the sugar predominating in the UK diet. Sugars have been considered in relation to a wide spectrum of human diseases and reviewed in the light of published evidence. Obesity as a risk factor for several other conditions (eg diabetes, hypertension) occupied a special position in these considerations. We have mainly considered observations and experiments in humans; animal experiments have been considered only when they appeared to have clear relevance to human disease. Artificial sweeteners have been considered to the extent that they might be used instead of dietary sugars.

1.4 Meetings of the Panel

1.4.1 The Panel was appointed at the end of 1986 at the recommendation of the Committee on Medical Aspects of Food Policy. It met ten times.

1

1.4.2 We wish to express our appreciation and thanks for expert assistance to the Secretariat. We are grateful to those who have prepared working papers and have made documents available.

1.5 Perspectives

1.5.1 Sugars in berries, fruits and honey have always formed part of the human diet. Sugars became a regular and substantial contributor to food energy intake in broad sections of the UK population only in the middle of the last century when large quantities of sucrose extracted from sugar cane (and later from sugar beet) became available in a cheap and easily transportable form. Sugars are the carbohydrate chemical units which, combined in chains, form the complex carbohydrate molecules which function in plants as a major energy store or in providing a rigid fibrous structure. Starch, the chief storage carbohydrate, is almost entirely broken down in man by the process of digestion to single sugar (glucose) units in which form it is absorbed.

1.5.2 The carbohydrates in the rigid fibrous structure of plants, such as cellulose, largely resist digestion but may be fermented to absorbable fragments by bacteria in the intestine. This poorly absorbed material makes up a large part of so-called 'dietary fibre'.

1.5.3 By contrast with these starchy and structural carbohydrates, sugars are soluble in water and taste sweet. They occur naturally in many foods, including milk, honey, fruit, vegetables and sugar cane and beet. Previously so costly as to be a luxury available only to the wealthy, cane and beet sugar (sucrose) has become relatively inexpensive and has been incorporated into the diets of all sections of the community. Sucrose now represents about one seventh of the average daily food energy supply in the UK (see Table 3).

1.5.4 With the widespread and increasing use of sucrose came claims that its consumption was responsible for the increased prevalence of a number of diseases including dental caries,[4] diabetes mellitus,[5] cardiovascular disease,[5] obesity[5] and behavioural problems.[6] These claims have attributed the diseases either directly to effects of sucrose on biological processes or indirectly to the loss of intact cell wall material ('dietary fibre') which occurs during the extraction, concentration and crystallisation process.

1.5.5 Most of these claims have been contested.[7, 8] For both the general public and informed observers, it has been difficult at times to distinguish between established facts and strongly held opinions. COMA felt in 1986 that the role of sugars in the UK diet required further clarification.

1.6 Form of the Report

1.6.1 We have attempted in this Report to derive practical conclusions from our interpretation of many lines of evidence. We have also tried to identify those areas where the evidence is inadequate or inconclusive and further research is needed. The data from which our conclusions and recommendations are drawn are summarised in sections 2–13 and the recommendations based upon them in Section 14. References are given in Section 15.

1.6.2   The recommendations were agreed by all members of the Panel.

2. The Nature of Sugars and Terminology of the Report

2.1 Sugars are soluble carbohydrates of fundamental importance in providing energy for the maintenance of life. Combined in chains they form an important food energy store (starch) and provide the structural framework (eg cellulose) of plant life. Plant life builds sugar units from carbon dioxide gas and water by the process of photosynthesis which uses light as the energy source. It is this incorporated energy which gives sugars their major nutrient property. The energy is liberated by regulated metabolic breakdown of sugars, either to meet current needs or to be stored, in animals after conversion to fat or glycogen (para 7.2.3). In this breakdown, sugars are ultimately converted back to carbon dioxide and water.

2.2 Glucose is the most abundant of the sugar units in nature. This single sugar unit is classed as a monosaccharide, as are fructose and galactose and many other less abundant sugars. Disaccharides such as sucrose, lactose and maltose are, as the name suggests, compounds of two monosaccharide moieties. Sucrose, the sugar most widely used as a food in the United Kingdom, is a disaccharide composed of glucose and fructose. Starches, the major carbohydrates in food, comprise a mixture of long straight chains (amylose) and branching chains (amylopectins) of glucose units and are formed by plant life as its energy store. Animals can construct long, branching glucose chains known as glycogen and this provides them with a readily available but relatively small and short-term energy store, the major energy store being fat. Starches in foods such as bread and potatoes as well as disaccharides are broken down by digestion in the intestine to, and absorbed as, their unit monosaccharides.

2.3 In this Report, the plural term 'sugars' has been used to include all the members of the chemical family of mono and disaccharides. When reference has been made to an individual sugar it has been named (eg sucrose, glucose, fructose). The most commonly occurring dietary sugars are listed in table 1 along with some of the foods in which they are found. Glucose is present in many foods, as the monosaccharide and as a component of disaccharides and starches. Lactose is present in milk and milk products, and sucrose, occurring naturally in sugar cane and beet and in fruit is added to many prepared and manufactured foods. Some sources of individual sugars in the diet in the UK are given in table 2.

2.4 Sucrose owes much of its sweetness to its fructose moiety, the sweetest-tasting of all the sugars. Other commercial sweeteners include glucose syrups and fructose which is increasingly used by itself as a sweetening agent and is prepared commercially by conversion from glucose produced by hydrolysis of starch.[2]

2.5   There have been many attempts to group dietary sugars; biochemically (monosaccharides, disaccharides, hexoses, pentoses, etc); in manufacturing terms (added, natural); in physical terms (extracellular, intracellular); or in dietetic and physiological terms. The last provides a more useful framework for the consumer, but is necessarily more complex in order to avoid misleading groupings. For instance honey though 'natural' acts as any concentrated solution of the simple sugars glucose and fructose. Milk sugar (lactose) is 'natural' and extracellular but neglibly cariogenic. Sugars in fruit juices are also 'natural' and extracellular, but have different cariogenic potentials and are more rapidly absorbed than those in intact fruit. We have attempted to produce a logical and comprehensive classification without inconsistencies for this Report which future workers may find useful. One disadvantage is that previous dietary studies used a variety of different classifications which are not immediately comparable.

2.6   It is helpful to distinguish sugars naturally integrated into the cellular structure of a food (intrinsic) from those which are free in the food or added to it (extrinsic). This difference in physical location influences their availability for bacterial metabolism in the mouth and the readiness with which they are absorbed after ingestion. The speed with which sugars consumed in the diet become available to the tissues of the body influences some of the metabolic responses to their ingestion, a question considered later in this Report. These availability classes have been defined as follows.

2.6.1   *Intrinsic sugars* Sugars forming an integral part of certain unprocessed foodstuffs, ie enclosed in the cell, the most important being whole fruits and vegetables (containing mainly fructose, glucose and sucrose).

2.6.2   *Extrinsic sugars* Sugars not located within the cellular structure of a food.

Milk sugars Sugars occurring naturally in milk and milk products (almost entirely lactose) are extrinsic sugars but the Panel considered them a special case so that they form a separate sub-group.

Non-milk extrinsic sugars Includes fruit juices and honey and 'added sugars' which comprise recipe and table sugars.

(i)   *Recipe sugars* Includes sugars that are added to composite dishes and confections. Recipes and formulations have a characteristic content of sugars, modification of which beyond certain limits results in a different product. Amounts of sugars in different recipes and products range from negligible (eg glazings) to providing 100 per cent of the food energy (eg 'boiled sweets'). Foods richest in recipe sugars include preserves, many soft drinks, sugar confectionery, biscuits, cakes and puddings. Without recipe sugars some foods such as gooseberries, rhubarb and cooking apples would rarely be eaten and others such as meringues, and various confections and desserts would not exist.

(ii) *Table sugars* Sugars, pure or reinforced with non-nutritive sweeteners, which the individual may choose to add to foods or drinks.

2.7 **Nutrient density** The relationship between the energy and the protein, vitamin and mineral contents of different foods, drinks and whole diets is of nutritional importance. The ratio of each nutrient to the energy content is termed the *nutrient density*. It is expressed as the quantity (usually in metric weight) of a specified nutrient per unit of food energy expressed as kilocalories (kcal) or megajoules (MJ) (1 megajoule (MJ)=239 kilocalories (kcal)). Since nutrient density is a ratio, it can provide information on absolute values of nutrient content only when total energy content is also known.

3. Technological Functions of Sugars in Foods

3.1 Sweetness of taste has given sugars their prominent place in human nutrition whether the sugars are intrinsic as, for example, in fruits and berries, or as recipe sugars added in domestic cooking or in commercial processing. In food manufacture the recipe sugars may be integral to the making of the product as in confectionery and meringues, or an essential component of the flavour of sauces or garnishings like tomato ketchup. Sugars, mainly sucrose, are added to jams partly because of their preservative properties. Sucrose is used as a bulking agent in cakes and is added to modify or enhance the flavour of foods and of drinks such as coffee and tea.

3.2 **Baked products** Sucrose has a major influence on the development of the characteristic structure and texture of cakes. It raises the temperature at which egg proteins denature and delays the gelation of starch, allowing the mixture to rise fully before it is solidified by heat. Glucose and fructose can be used as alternatives to sucrose, although greater quantities are needed to produce cakes of equivalent texture. Sucrose inhibits cake staling by resisting changes in moisture levels. Sugar is also important to the structure of biscuits. During cooking, the sugar dissolves, reducing the availability of water and so restricting the hydration of starch. On cooling it recrystallises and gives biscuits their characteristic crunchy texture.

3.3 **Chocolate and sugar confectionery** Chocolate is a suspension of sugar crystals (usually sucrose) and ground cocoa solids in cocoa butter. In chocolate the sweetness of sugar acts as a foil to the natural bitterness of the cocoa. Solid sugar ground so fine that the crystals are imperceptible to the tongue is responsible for the characteristic 'snap' of chocolate. In sugar confectionery, sucrose can remain in supersaturated solution with peripheral crystallisation, resulting in a 'sugar glass' characteristic of certain products.

3.4 **Diabetic and dietetic confectionery** A number of chocolate, cake, dessert and confectionery products have been manufactured using permitted bulk sweeteners (see section 13) instead of sucrose. These products are usually aimed at the diabetic market although some are used more widely, sometimes mistakenly, as slimming aids. Increasing numbers of confectionery products containing artificial sweeteners are likely to become available. Even without sucrose many of these products are relatively high in food energy. Consumed in excess some bulk sweeteners (eg sorbitol) have laxative properties.

7

3.5 Dairy products and frozen confectionery A principal use for sugars in dairy products is in ice-cream where they contribute to the familiar texture and lower the freezing-point. In soft-scoop ice-creams some of the sucrose is replaced by glucose and fructose syrups and glycerol.

3.6 Desserts Sugars provide sweetness and textural properties to products such as whipped desserts and custards. They have a preservative function in products like pie fillings through their ability to reduce available water and are widely used in compotes with acid-tasting fruits, berries and stems lacking natural sweetness.

3.7 Preserves The water sequestrating property of sugars at high concentrations suppresses the growth of some micro-organisms in stored foods. About 70 per cent of the weight of jams usually consists of dissolved sugars, and they do not therefore require artificial preservatives.

3.8 Soft drinks In some soft drinks, carbonated, still, or squash-concentrate, sugars are used to provide sweetness and an acceptable feeling to the mouth. Low calorie 'diet' drink alternatives using intense artificial sweeteners are becoming increasingly widely consumed.

4. Sugars as an Energy Source

4.1 Sugars currently contribute between 10 and 20 per cent of the food energy to the human diet in the UK. The technical meaning of the term 'energy' should not be confused with its popular use indicating physical vigour and vitality. It is often supposed that tiredness and fatigue (ie lack of energy in its popular sense) are due to depletion of food energy in its technical sense. Lack of vitality is sometimes ascribed to abnormally low blood glucose concentration (hypoglycaemia) but this is rarely the case. The argument that consumption of sugars or other energy rich foods will raise the blood glucose concentration and promptly reinvigorate the fatigued individual is false. In healthy individuals the concentration of glucose in the blood is maintained within relatively narrow limits. The availability of energy to the body is also regulated at a fairly constant level and, except in situations of starvation, is virtually independent of food intake. In the normally nourished person, recovery from fatigue will occur during a period of physical rest and is neither accelerated nor delayed by food consumption. Some of the psychological aspects of fatigue may be relieved by the diversion of a refreshing drink or taking food but this effect is not related to its energy content.

4.2 Food energy may be derived from many sources; the human diet is very variable in respect of the relative proportions of its carbohydrate, fat, and to a lesser extent, protein and alcohol content, all of which do provide energy. With a few exceptions people in developing countries obtain the majority, in some cases over 80 per cent, of their food energy from carbohydrate sources. In industrial countries with higher incomes, such as the UK, fat has progressively displaced carbohydrate as an energy source.[9] One of the principal recommendations of the COMA Panel on Diet and Cardiovascular Disease[1] was that this balance should be redressed by increasing the contribution of carbohydrate at the expense of fats, particularly those rich in saturated fatty acids. That Panel set the goal of reducing the contribution of fat to dietary energy in the UK to 35 per cent or less. Protein in foods, from animal and vegetable sources, contributes 10 to 15 per cent of daily energy consumption.[10] In some people alcohol constitutes an appreciable proportion of energy intake but its usefulness as a food is limited because of its adverse effects on health.[11]

4.3 Energy is released for biological use by the regulated oxidation of the fats, proteins, carbohydrates and any alcohol in the diet. The amount of energy provided by particular nutrients or by the diet as a whole can be determined directly by measuring it either as the heat released when it is burned in a calorimeter (making allowance for the combustible but non-utilised portion) or as the heat produced by the body following its consumption. Alternatively the oxygen consumed by the body for its oxidation can provide an indirect measure of energy used (see Appendix D).

4.4   Cellulose and other structural plant materials yield energy when they are burned in a calorimeter, but their contribution to dietary energy is very small. Starches and sugars are almost completely digested and absorbed and the factor used for calculating their energy yields in mixed British diets is 3.75 kcal or 16 kJ per gram of monosaccharide equivalent (see Appendix D).[12] The corresponding factors for protein, fat and alcohol are 4 kcal (17 kJ), 9 kcal (37 kJ) and 7 kcal (29 kJ) per gram respectively.

5. Intakes of Sugars in the UK

5.1 The use of sugars by the public can be estimated at four different points in the food distribution chain. The applications and limitations of each of these estimates are described in the following sections.

(a) *National food supply statistics* The Ministry of Agriculture, Fisheries and Food (MAFF) publishes estimates of the amount of each basic foodstuff entering the food distribution chain in the UK. This annual series, collected in a consistent manner for nearly 50 years, includes all foods produced in, and imported into, the United Kingdom and is the basis for international comparisons. Estimated deductions for exports and for non-human uses such as animal feed are made and the total further adjusted for changes in year-end stocks. The final totals divided by the mid-year population give an estimate of the supply, usually in kilograms per head per year. These estimates and their trends over the years for sucrose, glucose syrups and honey are shown in Table 3 and Figure 1. They include the sugar sold in packets, the sugars (apart from those naturally present in fruit and vegetables) later incorporated into cakes, biscuits, jam, ice-cream and other commercial foods and those which enter the catering sector. No allowance is made for wastage and the *per caput* estimates may thus be substantially greater than the amounts actually eaten.

(b) *Food industry statistics* Data on the sales of certain manufactured foods, including sugar and chocolate confectionery, are provided by some segments of the food industry. As with the Government's food supply statistics, they can give no information on consumption by specific groups of individuals such as children, nor by people living in different parts of the country.

(c) *Household purchases* MAFF's National Food Survey (NFS) has also collected information continuously for almost half a century on the amounts of all foods, apart from sweets and alcoholic drinks, brought into homes throughout Britain. A representative sample of some 7000 households each year records the quantities of all foods they purchase, including packet sugar and sugar-containing foods such as cakes, biscuits and fruits. The results are presented according to geographical region of residence, household composition, income group and other socio-economic descriptors but they do not show the distribution of food intakes among individual members of the household.

(d) *Intakes by individuals* Some dietary surveys attempt to record all foods eaten inside and outside the home by relatively small groups of selected

11

individuals. Although not always representative and rarely repeated, such surveys should nevertheless generate the best estimates of the amounts of sugar and sugar-containing foods eaten by those individuals. In practice there are biases of unknown magnitude. Food items may be left unrecorded, snacks and second helpings rejected because of the bother of reporting them; the survey may itself alter consumption, for example, by reinforcing a determination to restrict food intake.[13, 14]

5.2 **Sugars supplies in the UK** Figure 1 shows the daily *per caput* national estimates of sugars supplies in the UK from 1850 to 1987.[15–18] Supplies rose steadily up to the beginning of the First World War and increased again until the Second World War. From the low point during the Second World War (85.5g per head per day in 1943), supplies of sucrose plus honey and glucose peaked in 1958, when they averaged 147.5g per head per day contributing an estimated 18.2 per cent of available food energy (Table 3). Between 1958 and 1974 the estimate fluctuated between 137.6 and 145.4g (from 17.2 to 18.8 per cent of estimated total food energy). Since 1974 supplies per head have fallen and in 1987 stood at approximately 120.2g per head (or 15.7 per cent of energy). Within this total, glucose and honey supplies rose steadily until 1978 and subsequently decreased on a *per caput* basis but at a slower rate than sucrose (Table 3).

5.3 **Food industry statistics** MAFF estimates that almost half the sucrose moving into human consumption is sold as packet sugar and about half is used by food manufacturers. The major industrial use of sucrose is for the production of confectionery which accounts for about a quarter of the total used in manufacturing, while the soft drinks industry uses about one fifth.[19] Although the weight of confectionery sold has fluctuated, over the last 25 years it has increased by 16 per cent in the UK. The type of product has changed, with an increasing proportion of chocolate, rather than sugar, confectionery. At 34g per person per day, confectionery consumption in the UK in 1984 was the highest in the European Community.[20] Sales of soft drinks have increased five-fold in the UK from 52 to 259ml per person per day between 1950 and 1986.[21, 22]

5.4 **National Food Survey** The pattern of household purchases of sugar recorded by the NFS[10] is shown in Figure 2. Daily packet sugar purchases per head by households fell slowly from a peak of 75g per person in 1958 to 69g in 1970, then faster to 30g by 1987. This fall has been partly offset by an increase in soft drink consumption, estimated to have risen from 141 to 259ml per head per day between 1979 and 1986, corresponding to a rise from approximately 6 to 11g of sugar per day (MAFF unpublished 1988). People in income group A purchase less than half the sugar bought by those in income group D and by old age pensioners. Young housewives currently purchase less than half as much packet sugar as older housewives.[10]

5.5 **Dietary survey data** Some dietary survey information on consumption of sugars has been commissioned by Government, some collected for research and some for industrial purposes. The surveys differ in the type and size of population groups selected, and in the methods of dietary assessment. Some of the detailed information, along with additional unpublished data made available to the Panel and covering the period from 1960, is summarised in Tables 4–7. These relate to pre-school, school, adult and elderly age groups respectively. Details of food composition data used for these analyses are given in Appendix D.

5.6   Non-milk extrinsic sugars account for about half the total sugars intake in young children (Table 4) and perhaps a higher proportion in some groups of older children, adults and the elderly (Tables 5, 6, 7 respectively). In children of pre-school age, total sugars intake was 25 to 29 per cent of total daily energy consumption (Table 4) and was higher than that for schoolchildren (19.0 to 25.0 per cent, Table 5). The proportion was, in general, lowest for adults (Table 6) but among these was relatively high in a Dublin population sample of unemployed people (25 and 28.2 per cent in men and women respectively).[23] Among adults there appeared to be a trend for women to take a smaller proportion of non-milk extrinsic sugars in their diets than men, but the differences (in those studies which distinguished between the sexes) were small and inconsistent.

5.7   The main food sources of the intrinsic and extrinsic sugars in the diets of Northumberland schoolchildren and Cambridge adults are listed in Table 8. Table sugar, confectionery and soft drinks together provided 69, 66 and 58 per cent of recorded non-milk extrinsic sugars intake in children, men and women respectively. Biscuits, cakes and puddings accounted for a further 21, 16 and 24 per cent.

5.8   The Panel examined in detail the data of Nelson et al[24–27] derived from 7-day records of the dietary intake of 105 men and 112 women in Cambridge, England along with other available material. In particular they considered the quantities and proportions of sugars in these diets and whether these were associated with consumption of protein, minerals or vitamins so low as to constitute a threat to health.

5.8.1   The relationship between total energy intake and sugars and other nutrient consumption is shown in Table 9. Those people in the highest thirds of energy intakes consumed significantly more of all the nutrients, including sugars, than those in the lowest. Protein provided a somewhat smaller proportion of dietary energy to those in the highest total energy intake group (p<0.01); their proportion from sugars and alcohol was not statistically significantly higher, with the proportion from fat staying relatively constant.

5.8.2   Intakes of nutrients by people grouped into thirds according to the proportion of their dietary energy derived from non-milk extrinsic sugars are shown in Table 10. Those in the highest third consumed an estimated 8 to 11 per cent more food energy overall than those in the lowest, but this difference could have arisen by chance. Since total energy content varied little between these thirds, the proportions of food energy derived from fat and protein necessarily fell, the former from 42.4 to 36.5 per cent for the men and 44.6 to

13

38.0 per cent for the women, the latter from 13.8 to 12.0 per cent for the men and 15.0 to 12.1 per cent for the women.

5.8.3 *Sugars intake and nutrient density* The Panel considered the possible effects of higher levels of sugars intake on the micronutrients in the diet. The micronutrients shown in Tables 8 and 9 were chosen because Recommended Daily Amounts (RDA) have been set for them in the UK.[28] Intakes of zinc and magnesium are also shown, even though no UK RDA is set for them, because there is current interest in these nutrients. Taken together these selected micronutrients give an indication of the nutritional quality of the diet. Intakes of these and all the other nutrients for which data are available are given in full in Appendix E for information. The level of total energy consumption had little influence on the micronutrient density (Table 9). As might be expected micronutrient density was lowest in those diets selected for the highest proportional contribution of non-milk extrinsic sugars to total energy intake (Table 10).

5.8.4 The relation between intake of sugars and the composition of the diet at various levels of total food energy intake is explored in Table 11. This compares nutrient intakes in those Cambridge men and women with consumption of sugars above the median values of intake ('higher sugars') with those at or below the median ('lower sugars') within each third of the distribution of total energy intake. The UK RDA[28] are also given along with the US RDA[29] for zinc and magnesium. In general the intakes of all nutrients ran parallel with total energy intake. There was a trend for micronutrient intakes to be lower in those with 'higher sugars' than those with 'lower sugars' consumption within each third of total energy intake. This trend was clearest at the lowest energy intakes. Using the RDA as a benchmark, mean micronutrient intake appears to be low with low energy intake in general, but especially in women, much of whose low total came from extrinsic sugars.

5.8.5 Tables 11 and 12 show a reciprocal relationship at any level of energy intake between the proportion of energy in the diet coming from fat and that from sugar.[26, 30, 31] Restriction of dietary sugars would lead to a reduction in dietary energy unless it were accompanied by increases in consumption of other foods. In this situation the nature of these replacement foods will determine the change in the composition of the diet. People might choose complex carbohydrate or protein to meet this energy deficit, but a compensatory increase in dietary fat is an undesirable change[1] which could result from restricting sugars intakes. Tables 11 and 12 suggest that people who choose a lower sugar diet tend to choose one containing higher proportions of energy from fat and protein but similar intakes of starch.

5.9 **In summary:**

(1) On average people with high total energy intake eat more of all nutrients including sugars. (See para 5.8.1).

14

(2) At each level of total energy intake, sugars consumption shows a reciprocal relationship to the intakes of fats and protein[26, 30, 31] (Tables 10 and 11).

(3) Sugars intake is a weaker predictor of absolute micronutrient intakes than total energy consumption (Table 11 and para 5.8.4).

(4) At any level of energy intake a higher sugars intake is associated with lower micronutrient intake (paras 5.8.3 and 5.8.4).

5.10   The conclusions from the foregoing study of a Cambridge population sample are in general supported by other data made available to the Panel. There were similar findings in a study of pregnant women in Hackney.[32, 33] A similar analysis of dietary data collected from a sample of pregnant women in Leeds[34] (Table 12) also shows substantially lower micronutrient intakes in the lowest third of total energy intake with a trend to lower micronutrient intakes in those above median values for sugars intake in each of the thirds, most markedly in the lowest. Gibney and Lee (Table 13) report the daily food intake of unemployed families in Dublin.[23] There was relatively little difference in absolute values of micronutrient intake between the lowest and highest fourths of the distribution of table sugar consumption despite large differences in total energy intakes. The Body Mass Index (BMI) of the men with the highest reported table sugar intakes was substantially lower than those with the lowest.

5.11   The Panel concluded that those people who eat a lot of sugars also tend to have high energy and high fat intakes. At all levels of total food energy consumption the intakes of sugars and fat have a reciprocal relationship. Reduction in sugars intake might result in an increase in the amount and the proportion of dietary fats with a consequent possible increase in the risk of cardiovascular disease.[1] Sugars provide an acceptable means of contributing to the very high energy needs of some individuals. In people who eat only small amounts, dietary sugars may compete with other nutrients. For such people appropriate selection of food items is of special importance.

6. Sugars and Dental Caries

6.1 **The problem of dental caries in the United Kingdom** Dental caries is still very prevalent in the United Kingdom. In spite of increased use of fluorides, the decrease in caries prevalence over the last 15 to 20 years[35] appears to have slowed or halted in children.[36-38] In 1983 by the age of 5 years, 49 per cent of children in the UK had one or more decayed teeth, rising to 93 per cent of 15 year old children, with an average of 5.9 decayed permanent teeth per child.[39] The prevalence and severity of dental caries varies with geographic and social factors. Caries prevalence is generally lower in London and South East England than in other regions of the UK[39, 40] and higher in children from social classes IV and V than in those from social classes I and II.[39] Twenty-two per cent of adults of all ages have lost all their natural teeth[41] with at least half of the tooth loss caused by dental caries.[42, 43] More adults from social classes IV and V have lost teeth than adults from social classes I and II. Adults aged between 35 and 44 years with any remaining natural teeth have, on average, 19 of them decayed, missing or filled.[40] Adults suffer an average of three days dental pain per year.[44] In any one year a quarter of the adult population reports dental pain.[45] In 1987–88 the cost of the general dental services within the NHS in the UK was £934.6 million[46] the majority incurred in treating caries. This cost excludes hospital, community and armed forces dental services and private practice. Of the 410,000 general anaesthetics given within NHS general dental practice for dental extractions in the UK in 1987–88, 250,000 were given to children under the age of 15 years.[46]

6.2 **Aetiology of dental caries** As soon as a tooth erupts into the mouth, a dense layer called dental plaque, consisting mainly of bacteria, forms on the tooth surface. In less accessible areas this plaque remains undisturbed. Many plaque organisms metabolise sugars, generating local concentrations of acid in the inner layers of plaque, favouring local dissolution of the mineral structure of the dental enamel. When plaque acidity* lessens (or pH rises) remineralisation of enamel can occur. At first a loss of mineral causes whitening of the enamel, which subsequently gives way to a carious cavity, a stage at which restoration of the tooth usually becomes necessary. Most dietary sugars are easily metabolised to acid by plaque organisms. Some forms of dietary starch can be slowly broken down in the mouth to sugars by salivary amylase. These sugars can then be metabolised by plaque organisms to acids. Sucrose favours the establishment in dental plaque of *Streptococcus mutans*, an organism considered by some to be particularly important in

---

*Acidity is directly related to the concentration of hydrogen ions [H⁺] and is inversely related to pH defined as $\dfrac{1}{\log [\mathrm{H}^+]}$

16

caries aetiology.[47] In the majority of cases it takes several years for a carious lesion to become apparent, but a tooth can be destroyed by caries within months of eruption.

6.3 **Tooth development** Animal experiments have shown that high sucrose diets taken during tooth development result in enamel which is more susceptible to caries than normal enamel,[48] but this pre-eruptive effect is much less important than its effect on erupted teeth.[49]

6.4 **Evidence relating sugars to dental caries** The evidence relating dietary sugars to dental caries comes from many types of investigation. Clinical trials provide the best evidence but they are difficult to conduct since long term studies are necessary. Other sources of evidence include: human epidemiological and observational studies, human intervention studies, animal experiments, *in vivo* measurements of plaque acidity, *in vivo* enamel slab experiments, and *in vitro* incubation experiments.

6.4.1 *Human epidemiological and observational studies* A large number of studies have shown positive correlations between the level of sugar consumption, and the prevalence and severity of dental caries. These associations have been observed in comparisons between countries, communities or individuals. A high correlation was found between sugar availability and caries experience of children in 47 countries,[50] and many populations have experienced a rise in caries occurrence after an increase in sugar consumption.[51] People eating little sugars have low caries experience[52] and there were reductions in caries experience coincidental with wartime restrictions which included dietary sugars.[53] Positive correlations have been observed both in cross-sectional and longitudinal studies between caries experience of individuals and their consumption of sucrose or confectionery.[49] In contrast, diets containing high levels of starch but low levels of sugars are associated with low caries experience. This has been observed both in populations[51, 54-56] and in smaller groups of people.[52, 57-59]

6.4.2 *Human intervention studies* The Vipeholm study[60] showed that eating sugary foods between meals was associated with markedly higher risk of dental caries than when sugar consumption was restricted to meal times. In the Turku study, substitution of dietary sugars by xylitol in free-living adults was followed by a greatly reduced caries occurrence.[61-62] The intakes of dietary starch by the sucrose and the xylitol groups in the Turku study were similar and it can be concluded that sucrose but not starch was associated with high caries occurrence.

6.4.3 *Animal experiments* Important local (intra-oral) effects of sucrose have been demonstrated.[63] There is a positive correlation between caries severity in rats and the frequency with which they are fed a high sucrose diet, independently of the amount eaten.[64] Concentration of sucrose in food and weight of sucrose eaten are also positively correlated with caries development independently of eating frequency.[65-67] When the frequency of feeding was standardised, cooked starch or starchy foods (eg bread) have been shown to

17

be less cariogenic than sucrose.[68] Caries development increased as the proportion of sucrose in sucrose/starch diets increased.[67] Baked starch/sucrose mixtures are very cariogenic.[69]

6.4.4 *Plaque acidity studies* These experiments, which measure the acidity of dental plaque and not caries development, show that each time sugars are consumed there is a marked increase in plaque acidity.[70, 71] Cooked starch or starchy foods were less acidogenic than sugars or sugary foods when using the sampling method of assessing plaque acidity[72–74] but similarly acidogenic when the indwelling glass electrode method was used.[70, 75]

6.4.5 *Enamel slab experiments* In these experiments, slabs of dental enamel are mounted in intra-oral appliances which remain in the mouth while dental plaque accumulates. The plaque-covered slabs demineralise when exposed to solutions of sugars or sugary foods.[76] Two studies have shown that cooked starch or starchy foods cause about a quarter of the demineralisation of enamel slabs that occurs with sugars or sugary foods.[77, 78]

6.4.6 *Incubation experiments* Plaque organisms rapidly metabolise sugars to acids *in vitro*. Tooth enamel dissolves in solutions where the acidity rises above the critical level.[79] Unlike sugars, starch is not transported across the cell membrane of plaque micro-organisms[80] and must be split into sugars before it can be used by the cell. The rate at which this happens will depend on the salivary amylase levels and the nature of the starchy food.

6.5 **Different dietary sugars** Of the different dietary sugars, sucrose appears to be the most cariogenic. Glucose, fructose, and maltose may be only marginally less so.[49, 62, 70, 76] Lactose and galactose are substantially less cariogenic than other sugars.[49, 76]

6.6 **Weight of sugars consumed, concentration of sugars and frequency of consumption** Frequency of eating sugars and caries development are positively related.[60, 64] In animals there is evidence that the mass of sugars consumed and their concentration in foods are also positively related to caries development, independently of eating frequency.[65–67] In free-living people these three variables, mass, concentration and frequency, are all closely and positively related to each other. Caries experience is low where sugars supplies are on average less than 15–20 kg/person/year.[50] In 1987, sugars supplies in the UK were 44kg per person per year (Fig 1; Table 3) of which sucrose contributed 36kg.

6.7 **Sugars naturally present in foods** Although lactose alone is moderately cariogenic, milk also contains factors which protect against dental caries, so that milk without added sugars may be considered to be virtually non-cariogenic.[81–83] Fresh fruits, as eaten by humans, also appear to be of low cariogenicity.[84] There is no reason to suppose that natural syrups (eg honey, maple syrup, concentrated fruit juices) are not cariogenic.

18

6.8 **Dietary starch** From several different studies of the relative cariogenicity of dietary starch and sugars,[84] it appears that:

(1) the cariogenicity of uncooked starch is very low;

(2) finely ground and heat-treated starch can cause caries, but less than sugars;

(3) cooked staple starchy foods such as rice, potatoes and bread are of low cariogenicity in humans;

(4) the addition of sugars increases the cariogenicity of cooked starchy foods;

(5) in their natural state, fibre and phosphates in starch-containing foods may help to protect against dental caries.

6.9 **Non-sugar sweeteners** The permitted intense sweeteners (saccharin, aspartame, acesulfame K and thaumatin; see Section 13) are non-cariogenic.[85] Information about cariogenicity of permitted bulk sweeteners is variable; xylitol and sorbitol have been subjected to human clinical trials and there are substantial data on hydrogenated glucose syrup and isomalt, but less on mannitol. Current evidence suggests that bulk sweeteners have negligible cariogenicity compared with sugars[85] and that substitution of sugars by alternative sweeteners could substantially reduce caries development.[61] The greatest gain would be expected to occur if they were used to replace sugars in foods ingested frequently, such as sweet snacks, drinks, and liquid medicines.

6.10 **Groups of the population at greatest risk of caries** Dental caries can occur at any age. It is especially prevalent in pre-school children and has been associated with frequent and prolonged use of sweetened comforters[86] and sugared medicines.[87] The addition of sugars to feeding or comforter bottles containing fruit-flavoured drinks or milk is especially common in lower socio-economic groups and some ethnic minorities.[36, 88] Caries increases in adolescence,[39] and the elderly are at risk because of diminishing salivary flow and exposure of roots of teeth due to gingival recession.[89]

6.11 Sucrose is sometimes added to infant foods to prevent constipation in babies. Usually, all that is required to avoid constipation is to give more water. Rosehip syrups, blackcurrant syrups and various fruit juices have been widely promoted as vitamin supplements for babies but they may contain high levels of sugars. Sucrose-free vitamin drops are available at low cost at child health centres.

6.12 **Methods for caries prevention** Apart from reducing consumption of sugars the three other practical methods for caries prevention are plaque control, fluoride, and fissure sealants. Fluoride has been shown to be the most effective agent for caries prevention and is at its most efficient when incorporated in water supplies and toothpaste. Its use is considered the most important reason for the decline in the prevalence of dental caries in Northern Europe, North America and Australia.[90, 91] Plaque control (without the use of fluoride) is the least effective method.[92] Fissure sealants are effective but demand skilled application, costly in manpower.[93] The Panel recognised that caries had declined in the UK from 'high' prior to the mid 1970s to 'moderate' in the 1980s,[35] but considerable dental morbidity remains (see 6.1); the decline appears to have slowed or halted.[36-38] Even in areas of the UK where the drinking water has been fluoridated or has a natural fluoride content at the optimum level and with nearly all toothpastes containing fluoride, children with diets high in sugars still develop dental caries. In fluoridated north-east England in 1987, 50 per cent of 5 year olds had tooth decay, with 16 per cent of the children having five or more decayed teeth.[38] The protective effects of reduction of dietary sugars and the preventive influence of fluoride appear to be independent.[94-96]

6.13   The Panel concluded that the prevalence of dental caries in the UK is of social, medical and economic importance. The evidence relating dietary sugars to dental caries is very extensive and has been obtained from several types of investigation. Without sugars around plaque-covered tooth surfaces caries development is very limited. Caries risk can be reduced by non-dietary means, particularly the use of fluoride, but these methods can be expensive and are not completely effective. If the prevalence of dental caries in the UK is to be reduced further it will be necessary to reduce the amount and frequency of consumption of non-milk extrinsic sugars.

7. Metabolism of Sugars

7.1 *Metabolism* describes the many linked chemical changes which support the processes of life; it includes the transformation and breakdown of foods after their digestion and absorption from the intestine. Disturbance of any of the processes of metabolism may result in clinical disorders. In some cases this arises from the impact of a specific component of the diet upon the constitution of particular individuals.

7.2 Utilisation

7.2.1 *Digestion* The breakdown of dietary starches, higher sugars and disaccharides into monosaccharides in the intestine before absorption has already been described (paras 1.5.1 and 2.1). This breakdown is accelerated by enzymes secreted by the pancreas and cells lining the intestine. The sugar units so produced are then absorbed across the lining of the small intestine into the blood stream.

7.2.2 *Absorption* Sugars are carried across the intestinal wall by passive diffusion, by active transport or after breakdown to lactate within the cells. Sugars other than glucose and fructose are absorbed when their concentration in the intestine rises and they progressively diffuse into the fine blood vessels lying in the intestinal wall and so enter the circulation. Glucose and fructose are actively transported along with sodium ions into cells lining the intestinal wall. This energy-requiring process concentrates glucose and fructose in the intestinal cells to a level higher than that in the circulation, accelerating diffusion into the blood. The glucose and fructose absorbed may be metabolised to lactate in the intestinal wall and enter the blood stream in this form. Lactate is extracted and converted to glucose by the liver where it is stored as glycogen or released into the circulation for metabolism by the rest of the body.

7.2.3 *Metabolism of glucose* Glucose is distributed to the tissues where it fuels many chemical processes. Its energy is transferred in a finely regulated sequence of breakdown steps and it is ultimately converted back to carbon dioxide and water. Although fatty acids released from the depot fat can meet most of the body's energy needs especially under conditions of partial or complete starvation, the brain and nervous system have an obligatory requirement for glucose as an energy source. Maintenance of a constant blood glucose concentration in the face of variable or low dietary carbohydrate intake is achieved by continuous release of glucose from liver glycogen or by gluconeogenesis from amino acids, glycerol and lactate.

7.2.4 *Metabolism of fructose* Fructose is less rapidly absorbed from the intestine than glucose, but is readily converted to glucose by the liver which may release it or store it as glycogen. Some fructose directly enters the pathway of sugar breakdown and like glucose its fragments may be converted to fatty acids and deposited in fat stores or broken down to carbon dioxide and water. Fructose may also have a role in the metabolism of trace nutrients; in particular copper status may be compromised by high fructose diets.[97]

7.2.5 *Regulation of glucose metabolism* The concentration of glucose in the blood is normally held within remarkably stable limits, which provides an assured supply for brain function. This stability of concentration, maintained in the face of variable input from food and after prolonged fasting, is effected by the reciprocal interplay of hormonal and nervous stimuli. When circulating glucose falls too low, these stimuli trigger the release of glucose from liver glycogen, or, when it rises, promote its uptake by tissues and restrain its release from the liver by prolonging insulin secretion. If insufficient insulin is secreted or its action is impeded, unregulated release of glucose into the blood from the liver and reduced uptake of glucose from the blood by the body tissues leads to a rise in blood glucose concentration and the state of diabetes mellitus considered in section 9 of this Report. The state of hypoglycaemia, when glucose concentration falls too low, is considered in section 11. Reduced uptake of glucose by body tissues may lead to chronically raised compensatory levels of circulating insulin, a state of 'insulin resistance' which may be involved in disease pathogenesis (see para 7.3.1).

7.2.6 *Lactose* The principal sugar in human milk is lactose or milk sugar and is present at a concentration of 7g per 100ml in human milk.[98] It is also present in cow milk and most infant formulas. This sugar provides about 40 per cent of the infant's dietary energy and enhances the beneficial growth of lactobacilli in the gut. In adults lactose is a less important dietary sugar. Individuals who lack the intestinal enzyme lactase fail to digest it, leading to gastrointestinal disturbance (see para 12.5.1).

7.3 Metabolic responses to sugars intake

7.3.1 The ingestion of carbohydrates is followed by a sequence of hormonal responses and metabolic changes. Glucose and insulin levels in the blood are normally closely interrelated and regulated. A breakdown in this relationship is associated with clinical disorders such as diabetes mellitus and hypogly-caemia. Insulin has many other biological roles, including the metabolism of fatty acids, depot fats and proteins. Unduly high or low insulin levels may also be associated with the development of some pathological conditions.[99–101] There has been special interest in the effects of dietary sugars either directly, or indirectly through insulin responses, on the patterns of the fats (lipids) and on the concentrations of glucose and insulin in the blood because of their possible implications for arterial disease. Lipids (cholesterol and trig-lycerides) are carried in the circulation attached to specific proteins (the lipoproteins) and disordered patterns of the lipoproteins in blood have been linked to the development of arterial disease.[1]

7.3.2 The effect of experimentally altering intakes of sugars on blood lipids has been much studied in animals. While of considerable scientific interest these responses vary considerably among mammalian species and so cannot be extrapolated directly to man. The Panel considered that recommendations regarding sugars should be based on evidence derived from studies in humans.

7.3.3 Most of the studies in man have been performed on small numbers of participants and have been of short duration. The effects of altering dietary sugars depend not only upon the size of such alterations and the nature of rest of the diet, but also upon the subjects studied, their previous diet and their constitutional liability to exaggerated metabolic changes.

7.3.4 The relevance of the metabolic responses observed lies in their possible association with a number of common disease states. For example the higher the total blood cholesterol concentration, the greater is the risk of cardiovascular disease.[1] Dietary changes that raise the blood cholesterol level might thus be expected to increase the risk, while those that lower cholesterol levels to diminish it. Dietary changes can affect other constituents of the blood such as triglycerides and insulin and these may be implicated in cardiovascular and other diseases.

7.3.5 In a study in which sucrose was replaced isocalorically by complex carbohydrates for one week, blood cholesterol did not change when the replacement was based on bread and potatoes but fell when it consisted of leguminous carbohydrate.[102] Similarly, in a two week study in which dietary sucrose was replaced by potato and rice there was no change in blood cholesterol.[103]

7.3.6 A long-term study of the effect of replacing moderate levels of dietary sucrose with glucose for one year was carried out by Lock *et al*.[104] Inspection of their results suggests relatively little overall change in blood cholesterol although they claimed that it fell in the sub-group which at the end of the study was not found not to have gained weight. The two year Turku study in Finland[105] compared blood lipids, glucose and insulin in population groups consuming sucrose and fructose and found no differences.

7.3.7 When sucrose is eliminated from the diet, blood triglyceride concentration falls. Total cholesterol does not change appreciably [106–108] but HDL cholesterol may rise.[108] It is difficult to dissociate these effects from that of the accompanying weight loss. In fact when sucrose replaces starch isocalorically fasting triglyceride concentrations usually do not change.[103, 109]

7.3.8 When Crapo substituted fructose for sucrose in 11 normal people on a low fat test diet for 2 weeks, she found no systematic alteration in blood triglycerides, glucose or insulin although total blood cholesterol fell by 8 per cent.[110] In another study in people with initially high blood triglyceride concentrations a further rise was recorded in subjects adding 80g of fructose per day to their normally sucrose-free diet, but this was not sustained at 28 days despite continuation of the diet.[111]

7.3.9   The rise in blood glucose and insulin concentrations following intake of carbohydrate foods is related to the rapidity with which they are digested and absorbed. Thus, blood glucose and insulin responses to a food differ with the physical forms in which it is consumed (eg whole fruit versus fruit pulp versus fruit juice).[112, 113] This blood glucose response to a given food, termed its glycaemic index, compares the excursion of blood glucose following different carbohydrate containing foods with a standard oral glucose load. This index is better established for individual foods than for mixed meals or diets. Rapid glucose absorption is associated with higher insulin levels and this may be relevant to the claims that hyperinsulinaemia is associated with increased risk of various diseases.[101, 114–116]

7.3.10   Reiser has described a group of what he terms carbohydrate sensitive individuals who he estimates may constitute 10 to 15 per cent of the United States population. He defines them by their response of blood insulin to a sucrose load and they characteristically show exaggerated responses of blood cholesterol, triglyceride, glucose and insulin to sucrose intake than to equivalent amounts of starch.[117–120] These responses may be due, in part at least, to overweight.

7.3.11   In experiments on normal people whose daily sucrose intake exceeded more than 200g or constituted more than 30 per cent of dietary energy increases in blood insulin and lipids have been demonstrated.[121, 122] Since intakes of this magnitude are rarely achieved, these findings are of doubtful significance in relation to those with normal dietary habits.

7.4   **Thiamin and carbohydrate metabolism** The metabolic pathways by which glucose is metabolised by the body tissues depend on a large number of enzymes, many of which require co-factors and elements derived from vitamins and minerals consumed in the diet. The metabolism of glucose specifically requires the vitamin thiamin. It has been suggested that the thiamin requirement is 0.3 mg per 1000 kcal (4.2 MJ) of carbohydrate energy consumed.[123] With a normal mixed diet, the intake of minerals and vitamins such as thiamin increases with increasing total food energy intake. However the UK dietary pattern at present provides sufficient thiamin to meet the widely varying quantities of carbohydrate contributing to energy intakes.[10] Deficiencies are likely to arise only if dietary patterns are grossly disturbed as in excessive and continued alcohol consumption with restriction of normal food intake.

8. Sugars and Obesity

8.1   Obesity describes a state of excessive fatness resulting from periods when food energy consumption has exceeded energy expenditure. In this Report we have accepted the general, if arbitrary, definition of obesity as a Body Mass Index (BMI: weight (kg)/height(m)^2) of 30 or more. This does not take the distribution of body fat into account. Obesity so defined is associated with an increased risk for a number of diseases (eg diabetes, hypertension, cardiovascular disease, gallstones). Obesity and its related diseases all become more prevalent with increasing age[124, 125] (Table 14). This section explores the role of dietary sugars in the development and in the maintainance of obesity.

8.2   For the development of obesity the availability of food is a necessary precondition. Alone it cannot be sufficient as not all people living in apparently similar environments appear to be equally susceptible. Obesity tends to run in families.[125] Both genetic and environmental factors play a part in determining who will become obese.

8.3   It is very difficult to ascertain the long term dietary behaviour of individuals and we have only scanty information about the diets of people who later become obese compared with the diets of those who remain at normal weight. When people who are already obese are questioned they characteristically report lower total food energy intakes than lean people. However, this is unlikely to be representative of their habitual dietary behaviour because when estimates of energy expenditure have been made on obese people, it is greater than that of lean people.[13, 126–129] Reports of lower energy intakes in obese than in lean people may be due to unrepresentative behaviour patterns during the period of measurement.[130–133] They may be more likely to underrecord their intake than the lean, or they may be currently restricting food intake to reduce weight, their determination to do so perhaps being reinforced by the process of enquiry itself. In any case the food intakes and energy expenditures of people who have become obese may differ from those during the period of active weight gain.[134] It is even more difficult to relate the past intake of a specific food item such as sugar or fat to the development and maintenance of obesity.

8.4   Theoretically there are three ways in which sugars could contribute to obesity. Energy expenditure might be lowered by a high intake of sugars; the energy derived from intake of sugars might be specially directed to fat storage; or sugars could provoke overconsumption of energy containing foods. There is no evidence that sugars intake reduces energy expenditure. An effect by displacement of protein from the diet would be very small, of the order of one per cent or less of the total energy expenditure.[135] Nor is there

25

evidence that food energy derived from sugars is more or less likely to be stored as fat than energy from any other food source.[117] There are however *a priori* reasons for supposing that dietary sugars might provoke an increased food energy intake. Some people find the sweetness of sugars attractive[136] and this could promote in them the consumption of certain foods. Sugars are added to foods and dissolved in drinks which might otherwise be consumed without them (eg breakfast cereals, tea and coffee).

8.5   People with a 'sweet tooth' who derive particular pleasure or satisfaction from sweet foods might be thought particularly likely to overconsume them and so become fat. However, there is no evidence from psychological studies that obese people have a greater preference for sugars or sweetness in their food than those of normal weight.[136, 137]

8.6   As with total food energy intakes (see para 8.4) when samples of the population are asked about their consumption of sugars and their reported intake is related to their degree of adiposity, most studies report that the fatter the person, the less sugar they consume, an inverse relationship which is found even across the normal range of BMI.[130, 132] Many factors may operate to distort this relationship. Fatter people may have altered their diets, and cut out sugars; there may be systematic reporting bias and there may be imperfect recall of past eating habits. Although such studies fail to support the hypothesis that obesity is due to high sugars intake for the above reasons they cannot be taken to refute it.

8.7   The most direct experimental investigations of the effect of sucrose on energy intake were those of Porikos.[138, 139] In the first study sucrose was covertly replaced by aspartame in the diets of 8 obese subjects who normally obtained 25 per cent of their energy from added sucrose. In spite of access to unlimited amounts of palatable food, there was a 23 per cent fall in dietary energy consumption during the first 3 days of replacement, which reduced to 14 per cent in the next 3 days. The second study with 6 normal-weight male subjects, showed a similar pattern during 12 days of replacement of sucrose by aspartame. Of the scanty experimental data bearing on the effect of sucrose on energy intake these short-term studies are the best. Their relevance to people under normal conditions over longer periods remains to be demonstrated.

8.8   In studies in which a variety of dietary modifications included sugars restriction, several authors have noted incidental weight loss.[106–108, 140] Weight loss achieved by restriction of sucrose intake is probably not different from that which would follow similar restriction of any energy providing food.[141] Fat restriction may have a special role in the reduction of cardiovascular risk.[1]

8.9   The only controlled trial of the effectiveness of aspartame in assisting obese patients to lose weight is that of Kanders *et al*.[142] Half of a group of obese subjects who were recommended identical reducing diets were given aspartame sweetened foods and half were not. There was no significant difference in weight loss after 12 weeks. This small trial suggests that aspartame is not particularly effective as an adjunct to weight loss in obese people who are already dieting.

8.10   The Panel acknowledged the absence of sound evidence for a specific role for any single dietary constituent as a general cause of obesity. When sugars contribute energy to the diet they would necessarily be part of any total excessive intake. Although the arguments reviewed above indicate that sugars may favour food energy intake, the available evidence is insufficient to establish a link between sugars intake and the development of obesity. More intensive research into the constitutional, behavioural, environmental and nutritional aspects of human obesity is necessary.

8.11   Restriction of sugars intake alone is unlikely to be adequate to correct obesity and people seeking to lose weight should adopt this as part of a more general dietary strategy.

8.12   The Panel concluded that in obese people and those becoming obese, restriction of sugars intake is a sensible contribution to calorie restriction.

9.   Sugars and Diabetes Mellitus

9.1   The diabetic state is characterised by an abnormally high concentration of glucose in the blood (see para 7.2.5) and its loss in the urine, and is accompanied by many other disorders of blood constituents and bodily functions. It often leads to a characteristic pattern of damage to the kidney, the retina and lens of the eye, the peripheral nerves and the arteries—the so-called complications of diabetes. Diabetes is due to inadequate production or hindered action of the hormone insulin, which *inter alia* is centrally involved in regulating the storage, utilisation and production of glucose by the body. If insulin action is inadequate more glucose is produced by the liver and less taken up by the tissues for storage and metabolism.

9.2   There are two major clinical types of diabetes.[143] In the insulin-dependent form, usually starting in childhood or youth, insulin production by the body is grossly defective and insulin must be injected regularly to maintain life and health. The non-insulin dependent form, usually diagnosed later in life, is often associated with obesity. This form may respond to dietary treatment alone but may also require oral medication or sometimes insulin injections.

9.3   Although there are many other disturbances of the body's chemistry[144] the raised glucose is the most obvious and the most easily measured, in blood and in urine. Since excess circulating glucose is a cardinal feature of diabetes, excessive sugar in the diet might seem a plausible cause. The relationship of dietary sugars to the development of glucose intolerance and diabetes mellitus has been extensively reviewed. It has not been proposed that dietary sugars play a part in the pathogenesis of the insulin-dependent form of diabetes. The Panel therefore concentrated its attention on the non-insulin dependent form of the disorder.

9.4   The extensive literature on the evidence relating consumption of sugars to the development of diabetes was reviewed in detail by West[145] who considered both epidemiological and experimental data in man and the results of laboratory experiments in animals. The epidemiological evidence from studies relating sugar intake and diabetes prevalence in different populations and from studies over time in individual populations led him to conclude that 'in the aggregate, the evidence from these two approaches would appear to exclude sugar consumption as a dominant and universal factor'. This view was endorsed in the Report of the Food and Drug Administration's Sugars Task Force[3]—'epidemiological studies were unable to show a connection between high sugars consumption and diabetes'.

9.5   Experimental studies of the effect of dietary sugars on blood glucose concentration and insulin responses in man have, in the main, been short-term and have administered sugars in very large quantities and/or in unusual food mixes or 'formula diets'. Results have been inconsistent and difficult to interpret but do not suggest that a diabetic state is provoked by such manoeuvres. In the longest term study reviewed, blood glucose concentrations were closely similar when 30 per cent of the food energy intake was supplied as sucrose or as starch, each for a six week period,[118] though some elevation of the glycaemic response in selected individuals and higher insulin levels were found with sucrose in a more recent study.[146]

9.6   Animals fed diets very high in sugars may show rises in blood glucose levels. However, the quantities of sugar fed are so high (70 per cent of dietary energy in the highly inbred selected sub-strain reported by Cohen,[147]) or the interpretation complicated by accompanying obesity, that the application of these findings to disease in man is questionable.

9.7   The approach to diet in the patient with established diabetes has changed over the last decade. Carbohydrate is now proposed as the major source of food energy (50 to 55 per cent), which compensates for a decrease in fat intake to 35 per cent or less.[1] It is recommended that the additional carbohydrate should be largely unrefined, but compliance with such a diet may be improved by taking part of the carbohydrate as simple sugars. Intakes of sucrose up to about 50g a day taken with mixed meals as part of a diet high in complex carbohydrate and low in fat have no detrimental effect on diabetic control, at least in the short term.[148]

9.8   There are a number of foods sweetened with fructose and sorbitol which are marketed for consumption by diabetic individuals. Such products are not now permitted to contain more food energy than their conventional equivalents and tend to contain marginally less. Consuming more than 30 or 40g of sorbitol per day may provoke troublesome osmotic diarrhoea.[149] Fructose fed in large amounts has also been shown to have similar effects to sucrose on the regulation of blood glucose in the diabetic. Allowing limited amounts of sucrose in the diabetic diet further reduces the already limited place of these expensive 'diabetic foods' in the diabetic regimen. The British Diabetic Association recommendations allow up to 25g of sucrose as part of a prudent diet.

9.9   Non-insulin dependent diabetes mellitus is associated with obesity, and the relationship between dietary sugars and obesity is discussed in Chapter 8. The Panel concluded that there was no evidence supporting a direct causal role, independent of this, for dietary sugars in the development of diabetes.

10. Sugars and Cardiovascular Disease

10.1 There have been suggestions that the intake of sucrose is causally related to development of atherosclerotic cardiovascular disease.[5] Both a direct effect and an indirect link via obesity have been proposed. The relationship between sucrose intake and obesity has already been considered in chapter 8. Further consideration has been given to the possibility of a direct causal connection between sucrose intake and cardiovascular disease.

10.2 The strongest assertions that sucrose consumption was an important factor in the aetiology of coronary heart disease (CHD) were made by Yudkin.[150-152] His conclusions were based upon the arguments that

(1) reported national mortality rates for CHD in different countries correlated with their estimated sucrose consumption;

(2) the increasing mortality from CHD over the past 80 years or so has been associated with increasing consumption of sugar;

(3) men who develop CHD report a higher consumption of sucrose than healthy controls; and

(4) high sucrose consumption causes hyperlipidaemia and hyperinsulinaemia.

10.3 Many countries do not fit the pattern of high sugars consumption and high CHD mortality, particularly those in which high consumption of sugars is not associated with high fat intake. For instance countries like Cuba, Venezuela, Colombia, Costa Rica and Honduras have very high consumption of sucrose and low rates of CHD.[153, 154] Sweden with a higher sucrose consumption *per caput* than Finland, has a lower age-specific mortality from CHD.[155, 156] Further, a statistically significant relationship between CHD and sucrose consumption is not found when it is sought within countries.

10.4 There are anomalies in the comparison of national trends in sucrose consumption and CHD over the past half century. In the US, data from the Department of Agriculture show little change in average annual sucrose consumption. It was estimated as 51.7kg per person in the 1920's and 50.2kg in the 1960's, a period during which there was a marked rise in mortality from CHD.

10.5 Yudkin's claim that sucrose consumption was higher than normal in patients with cardiovascular disease was based on a study of 20 survivors of myocardial infarction and patients with peripheral vascular disease compared with a healthy control group.[157, 158] Dietary data gathered by questionnaire reported mean sucrose intake in the patients closely resembling the average *per caput* consumption in the UK. Their apparent excess intake was attributable to the unusually low sucrose intake reported by the healthy controls.

10.6 The possibility that sugars may have effects on serum cholesterol and triglycerides, risk factors for cardiovascular disease, has been considered in section 8.

10.7 The general conclusion of most workers is that Yudkin's hypothesis is unsupported by subsequent clinical, epidemiological and experimental enquiries,[157, 159] and that present evidence does not support any direct link between sugar consumption and the risk of CHD.

10.8 Similar conclusions have been reached by other expert committees who have also considered the evidence bearing upon this relationship. The joint FAO/WHO Report on carbohydrates in human nutrition[160] quotes the conclusions of Grande 'that a relationship between sucrose intake and the development of CHD is not supported by the available clinical and epidemiological data'.[102] A report of the Finnish Nutrition Committee[161] established to study the interrelationships of nutrition and public health concluded that 'no reliable evidence exists of the correlation between the carbohydrate content in the diet and coronary artery disease'. The Report of the COMA Panel on Diet and Cardiovascular Disease[1] could find no evidence incriminating sugar in CHD. The report of the US FDA's Sugars Task Force[3] concludes that 'no evidence was found to support the contention that current dietary intake of sugars contributes to the development of hypertension'; and that 'there is no conclusive evidence that dietary sugars are an independent risk factor for coronary artery disease in the general population'. The report of the British Nutrition Foundation's task force on Sugars and Syrups[2] concluded that 'there is no evidence of a direct association between sugars consumption and these other diseases (ie heart disease and non-insulin dependent diabetes)'.

10.9 The COMA Report on Diet and Cardiovascular Disease[1] recommends that the consumption of saturated fatty acids and of fat in the United Kingdom should be decreased to 15 and 35 per cent of food energy respectively and the ratio of polyunsaturated to saturated fatty acids in the diet may be increased to 0.45. Reduced fat intakes should be compensated for by increasing consumption of fibre rich carbohydrates (bread, cereals, fruit, vegetables). Even allowing for the difficulties in interpreting epidemiological studies in which sugars intakes varied along with many other cultural, economic and physical characteristics of the respective populations and the shortcomings of the experimental studies, the Panel did not find sufficient cause to make a specific dietary recommendation with respect to cardiovascular disease and simple sugars going beyond that in the 1984 COMA Report[1] that the consumption of simple sugars (sucrose, glucose and fructose) should not be increased further.

11. Behavioural Aspects of Consumption of Sugars

11.1 Sugars are popularly felt to have a calming or tranquillising effect; hot sweet drinks are often recommended to treat emotional or traumatic shock, but there is little evidence for any benefit. On the other hand it has also been claimed, mainly on the basis of anecdotal reports noted in reviews and commentaries on the subject,[162] that the consumption of sucrose by certain people may be responsible for disordered and delinquent behaviour.[6, 163]

11.2 One explanation offered for sugar-induced behavioural disturbance is that high sucrose meals overstimulate insulin production with a consequent depression of blood glucose to abnormally low levels (hypoglycaemia). It has been proposed that this may lead to brain glucose deprivation and to the release of hormones such as adrenalin to restore the blood glucose level, both of which might disturb normal thought processes or lead to altered behaviour.

11.3 In rare conditions in which blood glucose release from the liver is hindered, production of insulin may drive the blood glucose down to low levels (eg below 2.0 mmol per litre), but this process does not occur spontaneously in otherwise healthy individuals. Sugars may affect behaviour less directly by an insulin-mediated modification of the transport and metabolism of the amino acids tryptophan and tyrosine. These are the precursors of the monoamines (eg catecholamines, serotonin and dopamine) responsible for transmission of signals in the nervous system and which are thought to play an important role in the regulation of mood. In experimental animals administration of sucrose is reported to cause changes in brain neurotransmitter levels.[164] However no consistent effects on hehaviour have been demonstrated. The data on which a link between sugars consumption and abnormal behaviour is proposed are open to criticism. For instance abnormal psychological processes of some individuals could well lead to peculiar eating patterns rather than *vice versa*. The Panel concluded that there are no adequately designed and controlled studies in humans which convincingly establish the existence of a causal link between consumption of sugars and abnormal behaviour.

11.4 It has been suggested that sucrose consumption may be important in producing a 'hyperkinetic syndrome', characterised by restlessness and impulsive, demonstrative behaviour patterns. Others have asserted that sucrose aggravates symptoms only in children who are already hyper-kinetic.[165] The available evidence, mostly based upon uncontrolled unblinded experiments, did not convince the Panel of the validity of either of these claims.

11.5   Many of the reports of adverse reactions following consumption of meals high in carbohydrate and sugars describe symptoms characteristic of hypoglycaemia (ie sweating, shakiness and forceful beating of the heart). In some reports these symptoms are accompanied by, and in others consist entirely of, vague but disturbing psychological symptoms such as mood change, anxiety, depression, muddled thinking, and even aggressive or delinquent behaviour. The attribution of these symptoms to hypoglycaemia is often the result of diagnosis by unqualified individuals or by the affected persons themselves. It is rarely supported by the demonstration of low blood glucose concentrations, which, if measured at all, are usually within the normal range. There are, however, a number of extremely rare specific biochemical disorders which can result in hypoglycaemia, with symptoms which may include behavioural disturbance. In some cases, the symptoms are comparable to those induced by hunger and may represent normal arousal responses in hypersensitive people. Symptoms may be lessened by dietary change aimed to reduce carbohydrate induced oscillations in blood glucose concentration, through it is far from certain that such measures have specific effects.

11.6   The term Seasonal Affective Disorder (SAD) has been used to describe a condition in which recurring bouts of depression occur at a particular season of the year, typically late autumn and early winter.[166] During these depressive episodes sufferers are said to experience an increased desire for sweet, carbohydrate containing foods in many cases associated with substantial weight gain. It is claimed that 'carbohydrate craving' is due to a relative lack of brain 5-hydroxytryptamine, and that subjects seek carbohydrates to replenish this lack, thereby elevating their depressed mood.[167] The evidence for this is unconvincing, nor does it follow that sucrose has any consistent mood elevating activity.

11.7   **The 'Sweet Tooth'**   Infants like sweet things, an attribute demonstrable even in new-born infants of 30–36 weeks gestation.[168] There is a wide variety of items of diet that most children with free access will seek out and demand. In explaining the development of food preferences and in the genesis of the 'sweet tooth', experimental studies with human infants and children suggest that children tend to prefer and accept familiar foods and flavours more readily than new ones[169] and there is some[170] but uncertain[171] concordance between the likes and dislikes of particular foods within families.[172] Traditionally confectionery and sweet food have been used for rewards and celebrations which may add psychological and social reinforcements to later choices of food for consumption.

11.8   The Panel therefore concluded that the evidence that the intake of sugars as a cause of emotional or behaviour disturbance, either by provoking hypoglycaemia or by any other mechanism, is inadequate to justify any general dietary recommendations on this account.

12. Sugars and Other Diseases

12.1   The role of sugars intakes in a number of other diseases has been considered but there is only limited published material available upon which to base judgements and conclusions.

12.2 Gallstones

12.2.1   The majority of gallstones are composed of cholesterol monohydrate which crystallises with calcium salts from bile when their concentrations are excessive and when proteins are present which promote nucleation. Sometimes impaired gallbladder contraction plays a part.

12.2.2   Accurate figures for prevalence of gallstones by ultrasonographic surveys are available only for a few communities in Italy and Denmark.[173–176] Incidence data are not available. Autopsy and clinical data strongly suggest that gallstones predominantly affect people with western cultural patterns.

12.2.3   The relationship of obesity and raised plasma triglycerides, both risk factors for gallstones, to sugars intake has been considered earlier in this Report (paras 7.3.7, 8.10). A number of studies has examined the relationship between dietary sugars and gallstones. Some found a higher intake of sugars in gallstone patients[177, 178] while others did not.[179–181]

12.2.4   Sugar rich diets may increase cholesterol saturation of bile,[140, 182] but reduction in the intake of 'added' sugars (with the addition of bran to the diet) does not prevent gallstones from recurring in overweight patients after the stones have been dissolved by medical treatment.[183]

12.2.5   The Panel agreed that more data were required to explain the nature and extent of any relationship between sugars consumption and gallstones. Sugars may be associated with gallstones to the extent that they may contribute to high energy intakes, obesity and hypertriglyceridaemia.

12.3 Crohn's Disease

12.3.1   Crohn's disease is a chronic inflammatory condition of the intestine which chiefly affects the terminal ileum and colon and which often starts in young adults. Its cause is unknown but is probably related to the contents of the intestine; their diversion by surgical bypass usually improves the condition.

12.3.2   A number of studies have shown an association, perhaps restricted to non-smokers, between the occurrence of Crohn's disease and diets, one of the features of which was higher non-milk extrinsic sugars content.[184] A high intake of sugars has been shown experimentally, in the short term, to increase intestinal permeability[185] a non-specific finding which is an early feature of Crohn's disease.[186] However, there is currently no evidence for a specific relationship between the disease and intake of sugars.

12.3.3   The Panel concluded that the association between dietary sugars and Crohn's disease deserved fuller study.

12.4   Sugars and cancer

12.4.1   Nutritional factors are recognised as contributing to cancer risk.[187] Obesity has been related to cancers of bowel, breast, uterus, kidney and prostate. Only in the first of these has a specific role for dietary sugars been proposed.

12.4.2   *Colorectal cancer* Populations with higher energy intakes often have higher prevalence of colorectal cancer.[188] In the UK,[189] USA,[190, 191] and Australia[192] but not in France[193, 194] patients with large bowel cancer reported higher energy intakes than local control populations. Cancer of the colon is more common in overweight people.[195]

12.4.3   The intakes of protein, carbohydrate and fat are so closely correlated with each other and with total food energy intake that their independent effects are difficult to assess.[189, 190] In one study[189] 'sugars depleted in fibre' and combined with fat, contributed disproportionately to the higher energy intake of patients with colorectal cancer when compared with controls.

12.4.4   *Breast cancer* Breast cancer rates are higher in people consuming a 'western diet'[188] and in second generation immigrants reared on such a diet.[196] Breast cancer in older women in different countries correlates with the consumption of many nutrients, including sugary foods.[197] Obese women have an increased risk of breast cancer[196] associated with increased circulating levels of oestrogens.[198] There is no evidence of a specific role for sugars in the development of breast cancer.

12.4.5   The Panel concluded that there was little evidence of a direct contribution of dietary sugars to cancer risk. However, the link between some cancers and obesity and high energy intakes warrants further investigation of the role of individual dietary components, including sugars.

12.5   Sugars and Kidney Stones

12.5.1   Oral ingestion of glucose or sucrose loads may acutely increase calcium and oxalate excretion in the urine leading to the suggestion that the relatively high incidence of renal lithiasis in developed countries may be related to high intake of refined sugars.[199, 200] The increase in the consumption of sucrose (as well as of fat, meat and milk) that occurred in Japan between 1950 and 1975 coincided with a sharp rise in incidence of urinary stones.[201] These effects may be secondary to obesity, itself associated with increased risk for urinary tract stones.[202, 203]

12.5.2 The urinary calcium excretion rate in a group of men with renal lithiasis and their close relatives was significantly higher, on average, than that in 11 'normal' controls both before and after an oral glucose or sucrose load. There was, however, considerable overlap between the two groups.[204] Fasting insulin levels may be higher[205] and, after a standard oral carbohydrate challenge, the glucose falls lower[206] in stone formers than in control subjects. These responses may be indirect because stone formers tend to be obese.[202, 203]

12.5.3 Sucrose supplementation of the diet increases the urinary excretion of n-acetyl glucosaminidase (NAG), an enzyme produced by the renal tubules.[121] Patients with renal stones excrete more NAG in the urine than normal controls before and after challenge with cola and confectionery.[207] The significance of these urinary changes is not clear.

12.5.4 The Panel concluded that there was some epidemiological and experimental evidence linking urinary stone formation with nutritional factors including sugars intake. More investigation is required to confirm this relationship and the extent to which it is independent of accompanying obesity.

12.6 Inborn errors of metabolism

12.6.1 Deficient production or activity of one or more of the key enzymes catalysing metabolism may occur as the result of a genetic abnormality, inherited from one or both parents. Dietary sugars do not cause these conditions but the metabolism of specific sugars may be blocked leading to an accumulation of the sugar and its products preceding the block and a deficiency of those beyond it.

12.6.2 *Lactase deficiency* Lactose, the main sugar in milk, is broken down in the intestine by the enzyme lactase into glucose and galactose. As much as 75 per cent of the adult non-white population in Britain develop a degree of lactase deficiency.[208] If large quantities of lactose escape breakdown and absorption in the small intestine, this may cause bowel disturbances.

12.6.3 *Sucrase-isomaltase deficiency* This very rare defect results in deficiency of the enzyme sucrase which catalyses the breakdown of sucrose to glucose and fructose. Sucrase deficiency may first become evident in babies who develop chronic diarrhoea and fail to thrive after weaning to a diet containing sucrose. Exclusion of sucrose from the diet relieves the symptoms.

12.6.4 *Fructosaemia* This rare condition occurs when the liver fails to produce the enzyme fructokinase. If the next enzyme in the metabolic chain, fructose-biphosphate aldolase, is deficient then the major consequence is abnormally low blood glucose levels (hypoglycaemia) after ingestion of fructose. This is due to accumulation of fructose-1-phosphate which inhibits the production of glucose both from smaller molecules (gluconeogenesis) and from the enzyme catalysing the breakdown of storage glycogen (glycogenolysis).

12.6.5 *Galactosaemia* This is also a rare condition in which the liver fails to produce the enzyme glucose-1-phosphate uridyl transferase which is essential for the metabolism of the galactose moiety of lactose. As a result galactose accumulates in the blood causing toxic symptoms which appear soon after birth. The infant's urine contains galactose. Without immediate dietetic treatment death occurs rapidly. The infant should be fed special infant formula in which lactose is replaced by dextrins, dextrose or maltose.

13. Artificial and Alternative Sweeteners

13.1   Restriction of sucrose consumption is recommended for the prevention of dental caries and in the clinical management of conditions such as obesity and diabetes mellitus (see chapters 6, 8 and 9). Much dietary sucrose is added to food and drink by the consumer, so that its omission is relatively simple. Adjustment to the loss of sweetness is much less easy and for this reason, alternative sweeteners have been developed. Chemically synthesized or extracted from natural sources, artificial sweeteners are substituted for sucrose in many manufactured foods.

13.2   Non-nutritive sugar substitutes are intensely sweet, having from 30 to 3000 times the sweetness of sucrose. Most are excreted unchanged in the urine. Even if they are metabolised wholly or in part they make en insignificant contribution to total food energy. Sucrose, however, may contribute substantially to the energy content of some foods and drinks. For instance one can of carbonated soft drink has an energy value of about 140 kcal (577 kJ), derived solely from its sugars content. Replacement of sucrose in such products with a low calorie alternative is often part of weight reduction regimens.

13.3   Most artificial sweeteners in common use have some disadvantage, in taste (or aftertaste) or in stability during food processing. Different sweeteners are sometimes blended so that the limitations of each are compensated for by others. Sweeteners of different classes used in combination may have a synergistic sweetening effect.

13.4   A major question for any new artificial sweetener is its long-term safety. The Acceptable Daily Intakes, used by national and international regulatory authorities, are levels of intakes of food additives considered to be safe for a lifetime of exposure. Advice on toxicity, based on a scientific review of the available toxicological data, is provided by the Joint FAO/WHO Expert Committee on Food Additives. Progress towards a single market within the European Community in 1992 will require the harmonization of the laws of its member states in relation to additives (including sweeteners) in foodstuffs. At present four intensely sweet substitutes for sucrose are permitted for use in the manufacture of foods and drinks in the UK. These are saccharin, acesulfame K, aspartame and thaumatin. Cyclamate, although used widely throughout Europe, is not permitted in the UK.

13.4.1   *Saccharin* has been used commercially to sweeten food and beverages since the beginning of the century. It is 200–500 times sweeter than sucrose but, for some, has an unacceptable aftertaste. It is not metabolized and, being stable to heat, has a wide range of applications in food preparation and in beverages.

13.4.2 *Acesulfame K* is also about 200 times as sweet as sucrose, is not metabolized, and is very stable in many food preparations. When used alone a slight aftertaste is perceptible.

13.4.3 *Aspartame* has an acceptable taste, and acts as a flavour enhancer, particularly with citrus and other fruits. It is a compound of two amino acids, aspartic acid and phenylalanine. It contributes negligible energy to the diet and is 200 times sweeter than sucrose. It should not be used by people with the rare hereditary disorder phenylketonuria who need to restrict their intake of phenylalanine. Aspartame loses its sweet taste on heating, and so is used primarily in beverages and in foods that require little or no cooking.

13.4.4 *Thaumatin*, the most potent intense sweetener (2000–3000 times sweeter than sucrose), is a protein extracted from the West African fruit Katemfe (*Thaumatococcus daniellii*). The perception of sweetness is not immediate and is long lasting, leaving a liquorice-like aftertaste. It is unstable to heat, and is used in combination with other sweeteners in a variety of foods and drinks.

13.4.5 *Cyclamate* is the least potent of the synthetic sweeteners (30 times the sweetness of sucrose). Metabolized to a limited extent in the intestine (to cyclohexylamine), after absorption it is excreted unchanged in the urine. It is heat stable and so has many applications in food and drink production, often in combination with saccharin. Although banned in the USA in 1969 and later in the UK on the basis of limited evidence, it is in use in many European countries following the publication of more extensive experimental data. The use of cyclamate in the UK is currently under review by the Ministry of Agriculture, Fisheries and Food.

13.5 In addition to these non-nutritive sweeteners, a number of 'bulk' sweeteners are approved for use in the UK in foods often formulated for people with diabetes. These are modified sugars or alternative sugars eg sorbitol, isomalt, mannitol, xylitol, hydrogenated glucose syrups. All have about the same energy value as sucrose weight for weight, but insulin is not directly required for their metabolism. Sixteen per cent of the chewing gum sold is now 'sugar-free' containing sorbitol, mannitol and xylitol and approximately 30 per cent of syrup medicines sold in the UK are also 'sugar-free' containing sorbitol, saccharin and hydrogenated glucose syrup.

14. Conclusions and Recommendations

14.1   The Panel's remit was to review the evidence relating sugars in the diet to health.

14.2   The Panel found no evidence that the consumption of most sugars naturally incorporated in the cellular structure of foods (intrinsic sugars) represented a threat to health. Consideration was therefore mainly directed towards the dietary use of sugars not so incorporated (extrinsic sugars). Non-milk extrinsic sugars, principally sucrose, at present constitute about 15 to 20 per cent of the average daily food energy supply in the UK.

14.3 Dental caries

14.3.1   Dental caries remains prevalent in the UK. It is of social, medical and economic importance. Extensive evidence suggests that sugars are the most important dietary factor in the cause of dental caries. Their presence at plaque-covered tooth surfaces is essential for more than very limited caries development. Caries experience is positively related to the amount of non-milk extrinsic sugars in the diet and the frequency of their consumption. Staple starchy foods, intrinsic sugars in whole fruit and milk sugars are negligible causes of dental caries. Non-sugar bulk and intense sweeteners are non-cariogenic or virtually so. A reduction in the consumption of non-milk extrinsic sugars would be expected further to reduce the prevalence of dental caries in the UK.

14.3.2   Dental caries can occur at any age but those at greatest risk are children, adolescents and the elderly. Caries risk can be reduced by non-dietary means, particularly the use of fluoride, but these methods offer incomplete protection and some are expensive.

14.3.3   In order to reduce the risk of dental caries, the Panel *recommends* that consumption of non-milk extrinsic sugars by the population should be decreased. These sugars should be replaced by fresh fruit, vegetables and starchy foods.

14.3.4   Those providing food for families and communities should seek to reduce the frequency with which sugary snacks are consumed.

14.3.5   For infants and young children simple sugars (eg sucrose, glucose, fructose) should not be added to bottle feeds; sugared drinks should not be given in feeders where they may be in contact with the teeth for prolonged

41

periods; dummies or comforters should not be dipped in sugars or sugary drinks.

14.3.6 Older children need to be aware of the importance of diet and nutrition in relation to dental as well as general health. The Panel *recommends* that schools should promote healthy eating patterns both by nutrition education and by providing and encouraging nutritionally sound food choices.

14.3.7 Elderly people with teeth should restrict the amount and frequency of consumption of non-milk extrinsic sugars because their teeth are more likely to decay due to exposure of tooth roots and declining salivary flow.

14.3.8 An increasing number of liquid medicines are available in 'sugar free' formulations. When medicines are needed, particularly long-term, such alternatives should be selected by parents and medical practitioners. The Panel *recommends* that Government should seek the means to reduce the use of sugared liquid medicines.

14.3.9 Dental practitioners should give dietary advice, including reduction of non-milk extrinsic sugars consumption, as an important part of their health education to patients, particularly to those who are especially prone to dental caries. To facilitate this, the Panel *recommends* that teaching of nutrition during dental training should be increased, and professional relations between dietitians and dental practitioners be encouraged.

14.4 Obesity

14.4.1 Dietary sugars may contribute to the general excess food energy consumption responsible for the development of obesity. This condition plays an important part in the aetiology of a number of diseases, eg diabetes, raised blood pressure, hyperlipidaemia and arterial disease and gallstones (see Para 8.9).

14.4.2 Omission of sugars from the diet, though safe, is not usually sufficient as a weight reducing regimen. Restriction of fats in the diet is also important in reducing obesity and has other health advantages.[1] The Panel endorses the need for the obese to reduce energy consumption and *recommends* that the reduction of non-milk extrinsic sugars intake should be part of a general reduction in dietary energy intake. Overweight people who wish to lose weight and those becoming obese should follow the same approach to dietary energy restriction as that recommended for obese people. The Panel *recommends* intensification of research into the determinants of food choices and the mechanisms of the variety of individual responses to food intakes.

14.5 Metabolism

14.5.1 There is no evidence for a direct adverse effect in most people on blood levels of cholesterol, triglycerides, glucose or insulin when sucrose is substituted isocalorically for starch up to about 150g per day or 25 per cent of total food energy. A subgroup, possibly genetically determined and often overweight, comprising 10 to 15 per cent of the population, may respond with hyperlipidaemia to high normal intakes of sugars. At high levels of sucrose intake (about 200g per day or 30 per cent of food energy) substituted isocalorically for starch, undesirable elevations may occur in fasting plasma lipids, insulin and glucose.

14.5.2   A relatively small group of people with metabolic disorders may need to restrict or regulate their intake of particular sugars. This includes people with diabetes and those with certain rare inherited disorders.

14.5.3   For the majority of the population, who have normal plasma lipids and normal glucose tolerance, the consumption of sugars within the present range in the UK carries no special metabolic risks. Those members of the population consuming more than about 200g per day should replace the excess with starch. The Panel *recommends* that those with special medical problems such as diabetes and hypertriglyceridaemia should restrict non-milk extrinsic sugar intake to less than about 25 to 50g per day unless otherwise instructed by their own physician or dietitian.

14.6   Links between sucrose intake and certain other diseases (eg colo-rectal cancer, renal and biliary calculi, Crohn's disease) have been proposed. Although the Panel did not feel the evidence was adequate to justify any general dietary recommendations, it *recommends* the intensification of research in these areas. The Panel *recommends* that human nutrition should form an integral part of the training of medical students and of other health professionals.

14.7   The Panel concluded that current consumption of sugars, particularly sucrose, played no direct causal role in the development of cardiovascular (atherosclerotic coronary, peripheral or cerebral vascular) disease, of essential hypertension, or of diabetes mellitus (either insulin-dependent or non-insulin dependent). It further concluded that sucrose had no significant specific effects on behaviour or psychological function.

14.8   Artificial and alternative sweeteners can be considered non-cariogenic or virtually so and are useful sugar substitutes within limits prescribed by other Expert Advisory Committees. The Panel *recommends* that food manufacturers produce 'low sugars' or 'sugars-free' alternatives to existing sugar-rich products, particularly those for children.

14.9   Those wishing to regulate their sugars consumption need information of the sugars content of foods. The Panel *recommends* that manufacturers adopt current proposals for labelling foods including their total sugars content. The Panel further *recommends* that the Government seek the means for analysis and labelling of non-milk extrinsic sugars if practicable.

14.10   The Panel *recommends* that the Government should monitor average and extreme intakes of non-milk extrinsic sugars by members of the population in relation to the general and dental health of the public.

15. References

1 Panel on Diet in Relation to Cardiovascular Disease. *Diet and cardiovascular disease.* London: HMSO, 1984. (Reports on health and social subjects; no 28).

2 British Nutrition Foundation. *Sugars and syrups: the report of the British Nutrition Foundation's Task Force.* London: British Nutrition Foundation, 1987.

3 Glinsmann WH, Irausquin H, Park YK. Evaluation of health aspects of sugars contained in carbohydrate sweeteners: report of Sugars Task Force, 1986. *J Nutr* 1986; **116**: S1–S216.

4 Bunting RW. Diet and dental caries. *J Am Dent Assoc* 1935; **22**: 114–122.

5 Yudkin J. Nutrition and palatability with special reference to obesity, myocardial infarction, and other diseases of civilisation. *Lancet* 1963; **i**: 1335–1338.

6 Schauss AG, Simonsen C. A critical analysis of the diets of chronic juvenile offenders. *J Orthomolec Psych* 1970; **8**: 149–157, 222–226.

7 Sugar Bureau. *Putting sugar in perspective: dental caries.* London: Sugar Bureau, 1982.

8 Cocoa, Chocolate and Confectionery Alliance. *Confectionery in perspective.* 2nd ed. London: Cocoa, Chocolate and Confectionery Alliance, 1982.

9 Perisśe J, Sizaret F, François P. The effect of income on the structure of the diet. *FAO Nutrition Newsletter* 1969; **7:** 1–9.

10 Ministry of Agriculture, Fisheries and Food. National Food Survey Committee. *Household food consumption and expenditure: annual report of the National Food Survey Committee.* London: HMSO, 1949–1987.

11 Royal College of Physicians of London. *A great and growing evil: the medical consequences of alcohol abuse.* London: Tavistock, 1987.

12 Paul AA, Southgate DAT. *McCance and Widdowson's The composition of foods.* 4th rev ed. London: HMSO, 1978. (Medical Research Council special reports; no 297).

13 Prentice AM, Black AE, Coward WA, et al. High levels of energy expenditure in obese women. *Br Med J* 1986; **292**: 983–987.

14 Livingstone MBE, Strain JJ, Nevin GB, et al. The use of weighed dietary records and the doubly labelled [(^{2}H$_2$^{18}O)] water method to compare energy intake and expenditure. *Proc Nutr Soc* 1989; **48**: 21A.

15 Deerr N. *The history of sugar.* Vol 2. London: Chapman & Hall, 1950.

16 Ministry of Agriculture, Fisheries and Food. Food consumption levels in the United Kingdom. *Board of Trade Journal* 1968; **194**: 753–759.

17 Ministry of Agriculture, Fisheries and Food. Estimates of food supplies moving into consumption in the United Kingdom. *Trade and Industry* 1973; **9**: 459–466.

18 Central Statistical Office. *Annual abstract of statistics.* London: HMSO, 1976–1989.

[19] *Sugar*. London: Key Note Publications, 1982.

[20] Cocoa, Chocolate and Confectionery Alliance. *Annual report 1984*. London: Cocoa, Chocolate and Confectionery Alliance, 1985.

[21] National Association of Soft Drinks Manufacturers. *Soft drinks today*. London: National Association of Soft Drinks Manufacturers, 1985. (Factsheets; nos 8 and 12).

[22] Mansukhani R. *Soft drinks report*. 2nd ed. London: Euromonitor Publications, 1984.

[23] Gibney MJ, Lee P. Patterns of food and nutrient intake in the chronically unemployed consuming high and low levels of table sugar. *Proc Nutr Soc* 1989; **48**: 132A.

[24] Nelson M, Dyson PA, Paul AA. Family food purchases and home consumption: comparison of nutrient contents. *Br J Nutr* 1985; **54**: 373–387.

[25] Nelson M. The distribution of nutrient intakes within families. *Br J Nutr* 1986; **55**: 267–277.

[26] Nelson M. Nutritional goals from COMA and NACNE: how can they be achieved? *Hum Nutr Appl Nutr* 1985; **39A**: 456–464.

[27] Nelson M. *A dietary survey method for measuring family food purchases and individual nutrient intakes concurrently, and its use in dietary surveillance*. London: University of London, 1983. PhD thesis.

[28] Committee on Medical Aspects of Food Policy. *Recommended daily amounts of food energy and nutrients for groups of people in the United Kingdom*. London: HMSO, 1979. (Reports on health and social subjects; no 15).

[29] United States National Academy of Sciences. Food and Nutrition Board. Committee on Dietary Allowances. *Recommended dietary allowances*. 9th ed. Washington: National Academy of Sciences, 1980.

[30] Marr J. One man and his diet. *BNF Bull* 1986; **11**: 82–97.

[31] Black AE, Ravenscroft C, Sims AJ. The NACNE report: are the dietary goals realistic? Comparisons with the dietary patterns of dietitians. *Hum Nutr Appl Nutr* 1984; **38A**: 165–179.

[32] Doyle W, Sanderson M, Wynn AHA. Nutrient intakes of high- and low-sugar consumers during pregnancy. *Proc Nutr Soc* 1989; **48**: 46A.

[33] Doyle W, Crawford MA, Wynn AHA, Wynn SW. Maternal nutrient intake and birthweight. *J Hum Nut Dietet* 1989; **2**: 407–414.

[34] Smithells RW, Ankers C, Carver ME, Lennon D, Schorah CJ, Sheppard S. Maternal nutrition in early pregnancy. *Br J Nutr* 1977; **38**: 497–506.

[35] Murray JJ, ed. *Appropriate use of fluorides for human health*. Geneva: World Health Organization, 1986; 33–37.

[36] Holt RD, Joels D, Bulman J, Maddick IH. A third study of caries in preschool aged children in Camden. *Br Dent J* 1988; **165**: 87–91.

[37] Hargreaves JA, Wagg BJ, Thompson GW. Changes in caries prevalence of Isle of Lewis children, a historical comparison from 1937 to 1984. *Caries Res* 1987; **21**: 277–284.

[38] Rugg-Gunn AJ, Carmichael CL, Ferrell RS. Effect of fluoridation and secular trend in caries in 5-year-old children living in Newcastle and Northumberland. *Br Dent J* 1988; **165**: 359–364.

39 Todd JE, Dodd T. *Children's dental health in the United Kingdom 1983: a survey carried out by the Social Survey Division of OPCS, on behalf of the United Kingdom health departments in collaboration with the dental schools in the universities of Birmingham and Newcastle*. London: HMSO, 1985.

40 Todd JE, Walker AM, Dodd T. *Adult dental health. Vol 2. United Kingdom 1978*. London: HMSO, 1982.

41 Office of Population Censuses and Surveys. *General household survey 1985*. London: HMSO, 1987; 103–111.

42 Kay EJ, Blinkhorn AS. The reasons underlying the extraction of teeth in Scotland. *Br Dent J* 1986; **160**: 287–290.

43 Agerholm DM, Sidi AD. Reasons given for extraction of permanent teeth by general dental practitioners in England and Wales. *Br Dent J* 1988; **164**: 345–348.

44 Miller J, Elwood PC, Swallow JN. Dental pain: an incidence study. *Br Dent J* 1975; **139**: 327–328.

45 Cushing AM, Sheiham A, Maizels J. Developing socio-dental indicators: the social impact of dental disease. *Community Dent Health* 1986; **3**: 3–17.

46 Dental Estimates Boards for England and Wales, Scotland and Northern Ireland. (Personal communications).

47 Krasse B. *Caries risk: a practical guide for assessment and control*. Chicago: Quintessence, 1985.

48 Hartles RL. The effect of high-sucrose diet on the calcium and phosphorus content of the enamel and dentine of rat incisors. *Biochem J* 1951; **48**: 245–249.

49 Rugg-Gunn AJ. Diet and dental caries. In: Murray JJ, ed. *The prevention of dental disease*. 2nd ed. Oxford: Oxford UP, 1989; 4–114.

50 Sreebny LM. Sugar availability, sugar consumption and dental caries. *Community Dent Oral Epidemiol* 1982; **10**: 1–7.

51 Fisher FJ. A field survey of dental caries, periodontal disease and enamel defects in Tristan da Cunha. Part 2. Methods and results. *Br Dent J* 1968; **125**: 447–453.

52 Newbrun E, Hoover C, Mettraux G, Graf H. Comparison of dietary habits and dental health of subjects with hereditary fructose intolerance and control subjects. *J Am Dent Assoc* 1980; **101**: 619–626.

53 Soggnaes RF. Analysis of wartime reduction of dental caries in European children, with special regard to observations in Norway. *Am J Dis Child* 1948; **75**: 792–821.

54 Afonsky D. Some observations on dental caries in central China. *J Dent Res* 1951; **30**: 53–61.

55 Russell AL, Littleton NW, Leatherwood EC, Sydow GE, Green JC. Dental surveys in relation to nutrition. *Public Health Rep* 1960; **75**: 717–723.

56 Sreebny LM. Cereal availability and dental caries. *Community Dent Oral Epidemiol* 1983; **11**: 148–155.

57 Martinsson T. Socio-economic investigation of school children with high and low caries frequency. III. A dietary study based on information given by the children. *Odontol Revy* 1972; **23**: 93–113.

58 Hankin JH, Chung CS, Kau MCW. Genetic and epidemiologic studies of oral characteristics in Hawaii's schoolchildren: dietary patterns and caries prevalence. *J Dent Res* 1973; **52**: 1079–1086.

59 Kleemola-Kujala E, Räsänen L. Dietary pattern of Finnish children with low and high caries experience. *Community Dent Oral Epidemiol* 1979; **7**: 199–205.

60 Gustaffson BE, Quensel CE, Lanke LS, *et al*. The Vipeholm dental caries study: effect of different levels of carbohydrate intake on caries activity in 436 individuals observed for 5 years. *Acta Odontol Scand* 1954; **11**: 232–364.

61 Scheinin A, Mäkinen KK. Turku sugar studies I–XXI. *Acta Odontol Scand* 1975; **33**: 1–349.

62 Scheinin A. Influence of the diagnostic level on caries incidence in two controlled clinical trials. *Caries Res* 1979; **13**: 91.

63 Kite OW, Shaw JH, Soggnaes RF. The prevention of experimental tooth decay by tube-feeding. *J Nutr* 1950; **42**: 89–105.

64 Konig KG, Schmid P, Schmid R. An apparatus for frequency-controlled feeding of small rodents and its use in dental caries experiments. *Arch Oral Biol* 1968; **13**: 13–26.

65 Mikx FHM, Van der Hoeven JS, Plasschaert AJM, Konig KG. Effect of *Actinomyces viscosus* on the establishment and symbiosis of *Streptococcus mutans* and *Streptococcus sanguis* in SPF rats on different sucrose diets. *Caries Res* 1975; **9**: 1–20.

66 Huxley HG. The cariogenicity of dietary sucrose at various levels in two strains of rat under unrestricted and controlled-frequency feeding conditions. *Caries Res* 1977; **11**: 237–242.

67 Hefti A, Schmid R. Effect on caries incidence in rats of increasing dietary sucrose levels. *Caries Res* 1979; **13**: 298–300.

68 Konig KG. Caries activity induced by frequency-controlled feeding of diets containing sucrose or bread to Osborne-Mendel rats. *Arch Oral Biol* 1969; **14**: 991–993.

69 Grenby TH, Paterson FM. Effect of sweet biscuits on the incidence of dental caries in rats. *Br J Nutr* 1972; **27**: 195–199.

70 Imfeld TN. *Identification of low caries risk dietary components*. Basel: Karger, 1983.

71 Edgar WM. Prediction of the cariogenicity of various foods. *Int Dent J* 1985; **35**: 190–194.

72 Frostell G. Effect of a cooked starch solution on the pH of dental plaque. *Swed Dent J* 1972; **65**: 161–165.

73 Edgar WM, Bibby BG, Mundorff S, Rowley J. Acid production in plaque after eating snacks: modifying factors in foods. *J Am Dent Assoc* 1975; **90**: 418–425.

74 Rugg-Gunn AJ, Edgar WM, Jenkins GN. The effect of eating some British snacks upon the pH of human dental plaque. *Br Dent J* 1978; **145**: 95–100.

75 Schachtele CF, Jensen ME. Human plaque pH studies: estimating the acidogenic potential of foods. Cereal Foods World 1981; **26**: 14–18.

76 Koulourides T, Bodden R, Keller S, Manson-Hing L, Lastra J, Housch T. Cariogenicity of nine sugars tested with an intraoral device in man. *Caries Res* 1976; **10**: 427–441.

77 Thomson ME, Pearce EIF. The cariogenicity of experimental biscuits containing wheatgerm and rolled oats, and the effect of supplementation with milk powder. *N Z Dent J* 1982; **78**: 3–6.

[78] Brudevold F, Goulet D, Tehrani A, Attarzadeh F, Van Houte J. Intraoral demineralization and maltose clearance from wheat starch. *Caries Res* 1985; **19**: 136–144.

[79] Jenkins GN. *The physiology and biochemistry of the mouth*. 4th ed. Oxford: Blackwell, 1978.

[80] Birkhed D, Skude G. Relation of amylase to starch and lycasin metabolism in human dental plaque in vitro. *Scand J Dent Res* 1978; **86**: 248–258.

[81] Jenkins GN, Ferguson PS. Milk and dental caries. *Br Dent J* 1966; **120**: 472–477.

[82] Storey E. Milk and dental decay. In: Storey E, ed. *Diet and dental disease*. Melbourne: University of Melbourne, 1982; 34–41.

[83] Rugg-Gunn AJ, Roberts GJ, Wright WG. Effect of human milk on plaque pH in situ and enamel dissolution in vitro compared with bovine milk, lactose, and sucrose. *Caries Res* 1985; **19**: 327–334.

[84] Rugg-Gunn AJ. *Starchy foods and fresh fruits: their relative importance as a source of dental caries in Britain*. London: Health Education Council, 1986. (Occasional paper; no 3).

[85] Rugg-Gunn AJ, Edgar WM. Sweeteners and dental health. *Community Dent Health* 1985; **2**: 213–223.

[86] Winter GB. Problems involved with the use of comforters. *Int Dent J* 1980; **30**: 28–38.

[87] Hobson P. Sugar based medicines and dental disease. *Community Dent Health* 1985; **2**: 57–62.

[88] Silver DH. A longitudinal study of infant feeding practice, diet and caries, related to social class in children aged 3 and 8–10 years. *Br Dent J* 1987; **163**: 296–300.

[89] Rugg-Gunn AJ. Practical aspects of diet and dental caries in the elderly. In: Derrick DD, ed. *The dental annual*. Bristol: Wright, 1985; 159–165.

[90] Glass RL. The first international conference on the declining prevalence of dental caries. *J Dent Res* 1982; **61**: 1304–1383.

[91] Fédération Dentaire Internationale/World Health Organisation Joint Working Group 5. Changing patterns of oral health and implications for oral health manpower. Part 1. *Int Dent J* 1985; **35**: 235–251.

[92] Sutcliffe P. Oral cleanliness and dental caries. In: Murray JJ, ed. *The prevention of dental disease*. Oxford: Oxford UP, 1983; 159–174.

[93] British Dental Association/Department of Health and Social Security Joint Working Party. Fissure sealants: report of the joint BDA/DHSS working party. *Br Dent J* 1986; **161**: 343–344.

[94] Weaver R. Fluorine and war-time diet. *Br Dent J* 1950; **88**: 231–239.

[95] Granath LE, Rootzén H, Liljegren E, Holst K, Köhler L. Variation in caries prevalence related to combinations of dietary and oral hygiene habits and chewing fluoride tablets in 4-year-old children. *Caries Res* 1978; **12**: 83–92.

[96] Kunzel W. Fluoridation in relation to dental health. In: Rugg-Gunn AJ, Rahmatulla M, eds. *New frontiers in fluoride studies for health*. Singapore: COSTED, 1988: 31–51.

97 Reiser S, Smith JC, Mertz W, *et al.* Indices of copper status in humans consuming a typical American diet containing either fructose or starch. *Am J Clin Nutr* 1985; **42**: 242–251.

98 Department of Health and Social Security. *Present day practice in infant feeding: third report.* London: HMSO, 1988. (Reports on health and social subjects; no 32).

99 Jarrett RJ, McCartney P, Keen H. The Bedford survey: ten year mortality rates in newly diagnosed diabetics, borderline diabetics and normoglycaemic controls and risk indices for coronary heart disease in borderline diabetics. *Diabetologia* 1982; **22**: 79–84.

100 Stout RW. Insulin and atheroma: an update. *Lancet* 1987; **i**: 1077–1079.

101 Modan M, Halkin H, Fuchs Z, *et al.* Hyperinsulinaemia—a link between glucose tolerance, obesity, hypertension, dislipoproteinemia, elevated serum uric acid and internal cation balance. *Diabetes and, Metabolism* 1987; **13**: 375–380.

102 Grande F, Anderson JT, Keys A. Effect of carbohydrates of leguminous seeds, wheat and potatoes on serum cholesterol concentration in man. *J Nutr* 1965; **86**: 313–317.

103 Mann JI, Truswell AS. Effects of isocaloric exchange of dietary sucrose and starch on fasting serum lipids, postprandial insulin secretion and alimentary lipaemia in human subjects. *Br J Nutr* 1972; **27**: 395–405.

104 Lock S, Ford MA, Bagley R, Green LF. The effect on plasma lipids of the isoenergetic replacement of table sucrose by dried glucose syrup (maize-syrup solids) in the normal diet of adult men over a period of 1 year. *Br J Nutr* 1980; **43**: 251–256.

105 Mäkinen KK, Scheinin A. Turku sugar studies XI: effect of sucrose, fructose and xylitol diets on glucose, lipid and urate metabolism. *Acta Odontol Scand* 1975; **33**: 239–245.

106 Mann JI, Truswell AS, Hendricks DA, Manning E. Effects on serum-lipids in normal men of reducing dietary sucrose or starch for five months. *Lancet* 1970; **i**: 870–872.

107 Rifkind BM, Lawson DH, Gale M. Effect of short-term sucrose restriction on serum-lipid levels. *Lancet* 1966; **ii**: 1379–1381.

108 Werner D, Emmett PM, Heaton KW. Effects of dietary sucrose on factors influencing cholesterol gall stone formation. *Gut* 1984; **25**: 269–274.

109 Mann JI, Truswell AS, Manning EB, Randles J. Effects of omitting dietary sucrose and isoenergetic substitution of starch in primary type IV hyperlipoproteinaemia. *Proc Nutr Soc* 1974; **33**: 2A–3A.

110 Crapo PA, Kolterman OG. The metabolic effects of 2-week fructose feeding in normal subjects. *Am J Clin Nutr* 1984; **39**: 525–534.

111 Cybulska S, Naruszewicz M. The effect of short-term and prolonged fructose intake on VLDL-TG and relative properties on apo CIII1 and apo CII in the VLDL fraction in type IV hyperlipoproteinaemia. *Nährung* 1982; **26**: 253–261.

112 Haber GB, Heaton KW, Murphy D, Burroughs LF. Depletion and disruption of dietary fibre: effects on satiety, plasma-glucose and serum-insulin. *Lancet* 1977; **ii**: 679–682.

113 Bolton RP, Heaton KW, Burroughs LF. The role of dietary fibre in satiety, glucose, and insulin: studies with fruit and fruit juice. *Am J Clin Nutr* 1981; **34**: 211–217.

114 Stout RW. Diabetes and atherosclerosis—the role of insulin. *Diabetologia* 1979; **16**: 141–150.

115 Pyorala K, Savolainen E, Kaukola S, Haapakoski J. High plasma insulin as a coronary heart disease risk factor. In: Eschwege E, ed. *Advances in diabetes epidemiology: proceedings of the International Symposium on the Advances in Diabetes Epidemiology, Abbaye de Fontevraud, France, 3–7 May 1982*. Amsterdam: Elsevier, 1983; 143–148. (INSERM symposium series: no 22).

116 Jarrett RJ. Is insulin atherogenic? *Diabetologia* 1988; **31**: 71–75.

117 Reiser S, Hallfrisch J, Michaelis OE, Lazar FL, Martin RE, Prather ES. Isocaloric exchange of dietary starch and sucrose in humans. I. Effects on levels of fasting blood lipids. *Am J Clin Nutr* 1979; **32**: 1659–1669.

118 Reiser S, Handler HB, Gardner LB, Hallfrisch JG, Michaelis OE, Prather ES. Isocaloric exchange of dietary starch and sucrose in humans. II. Effect on fasting blood insulin, glucose, and glucagon and on insulin and glucose response to a sucrose load. *Am J Clin Nutr* 1979; **32**: 2206–2216.

119 Reiser S, Bohn E, Hallfrisch J, Michaelis OE, Keeney M, Prather ES. Serum insulin and glucose in hyperinsulinemic subjects fed three different levels of sucrose. *Am J Clin Nutr* 1981; **34**: 2348–2358.

120 Reiser S, Bickard NC, Hallfrisch J, Michaelis OE, Prather ES. Blood lipids and their distribution in lipoproteins in hyperinsulinemic subjects fed three different levels of sucrose. *J Nutr* 1981; **111**: 1045–1057.

121 Yudkin J, Kang SS, Bruckdorfer KR. Effect of high dietary sugar. *Br Med J* 1980; **281**: 1396.

122 Macdonald I. Interrelationship between the influences of dietary carbohydrates and fats on fasting serum lipids. *Am J Clin Nutr* 1967; **20**: 345–351.

123 Sauberlich HE, Skala, JH, Dowdy RP. *Laboratory tests for the assessment of nutritional status*. Cleveland: CRC Press, 1974.

124 Knight I. *The heights and weights of adults in Great Britain: report of a survey carried out on behalf of the Department of Health and Social Security covering adults aged 16–64*. London: HMSO, 1984.

125 Garrow JS. *Obesity and related diseases*. Edinburgh: Churchill Livingstone, 1988.

126 Ravussin E, Burnand B, Schutz Y, Jéquier E. Twenty-four-hour energy expenditure and resting metabolic rate in obese, moderately obese and control subjects. *Am J Clin Nutr* 1982; **35**: 566–573.

127 Blaza S, Garrow JS. Thermogenic response to temperature, exercise and food stimuli in lean and obese women, studies by 24 h direct calorimetry. *Br J Nutr* 1983; **49**: 171–180.

128 Schutz Y, Jéquier E. Energy expenditure [Letter]. *Lancet* 1986; **i**: 101–102.

129 Blair D, Buskirk ER. Habitual daily energy expenditure and activity levels of lean and adult-onset and child-onset obese women. *Am J Clin Nutr* 1987; **45**: 540–550.

130 Richardson JF. The sugar intake of businessmen and its inverse relationship with relative weight. *Br J Nutr* 1972; **27**: 449–460.

131 Kannel WB, Gordon T. Some determinants of obesity and its impact as a cardiovascular risk factor. In: Howard A, ed. *Recent advances in obesity research. 1. Proceedings of the First International Congress on Obesity, 8–11 October 1974, held at the Royal College of Physicians, London*. London: Newman, 1975; 14–27.

132 Keen H, Thomas BJ, Jarrett RJ, Fuller JH. Nutrient intake, adiposity, and diabetes. *Br Med J* 1979; **i**: 655–658.

133 Romieu I, Willett WC, Stampfer NJ, *et al*. Energy intake and other determinants of relative weight. *Am J Clin Nutr* 1988; **47**: 406–412.

134 Ravussin E, Lillioja S, Knowler WC, *et al*. Reduced rate of energy expenditure as a risk factor for body-weight gain. *New Engl J Med* 1988; **318**: 467–472.

135 Nair KS, Halliday D, Garrow JS. Thermic response to isoenergetic protein, carbohydrate or fat meals in lean and obese subjects. *Clin Sci* 1983; **65**: 307–312.

136 Drenowski A, Brunzell JD, Sande K, Iverius PH, Greenwood MRC. Sweet tooth reconsidered: taste responsiveness in human obesity. *Physiol Behav* 1985; **35**: 617–622.

137 Grinker J. Obesity and taste: sensory and cognitive factors in food intake. In: Bray G, ed. *Obesity in perspective: a conference sponsored by the John E Fogarty International Center for Advanced Study in the Health Sciences, National Institutes of Health, Bethesda, Md, October 1–3, 1973*. Washington: Government Printing Office, 1973; 73–80.

138 Porikos KP, Booth G, Van Itallie TB. Effect of covert nutritive dilution on the spontaneous food intake of obese individuals: a pilot study. *Am J Clin Nutr* 1977; **30**: 1638–1644.

139 Porikos KP, Hesser MF, Van Itallie TB. Caloric regulation in normal-weight men maintained on a palatable diet of conventional foods. *Physiol Behav* 1982; **29**: 293–300.

140 Thornton JR, Emmett PM, Heaton KW. Diet and gall stones: effects of refined and unrefined carbohydrate diets on bile cholesterol saturation and bile acid metabolism. *Gut* 1983; **24**: 2–6.

141 Lissner L, Levitsky DA, Strupp BJ, Kalkwarf HJ, Roe DA. Dietary fat and the regulation of energy intake in human subjects. *Am J Clin Nutr* 1987; **46**: 886–892.

142 Kanders BS, Lavin PT, Kowalchuk MB, Greenberg I, Blackburn GL. An evaluation of the effect of aspartame on weight loss. *Appetite* 1988; **11**: 73–84.

143 World Health Organization. *Diabetes mellitus: report of a WHO study group*. Geneva: World Health Organization, 1985. (Technical report series; no 727).

144 Alberti KGMM. Blood metabolites in the diagnosis and treatment of diabetes mellitus. *Postgrad Med J* 1973; **49**: 955–963.

145 West KM. *Epidemiology of diabetes and its vascular lesions*. New York: Elsevier, 1978.

146 Reiser S, Hallfrisch J, Fields M, *et al*. Effects of sugars on indices of glucose tolerance in humans. *Am J Clin Nutr* 1986; **43**: 151–159.

147 Cohen AM. Effect of sucrose feeding on glucose tolerance. *Acta Med Scand* 1972; **542**: 173–179.

148 Peterson DB, Lambert J, Gerring S, *et al*. Sucrose in the diabetic diet—just another carbohydrate? *Diabetic Med* 1986; **2**: 345–347.

149 Ministry of Agriculture, Fisheries and Food. Food Additives and Contaminants Committee. *Report on the review of sweeteners in foods*. London: HMSO, 1982.

150 Yudkin J. Diet and coronary thrombosis: hypothesis and fact. *Lancet* 1957; **ii**: 155–162.

151 Yudkin J. Dietary fat and dietary sugar in relation to ischaemic heart-disease and diabetes. *Lancet* 1964; **ii**: 4–5.

152 Yudkin J. Sugar consumption and myocardial infarction [Letter]. *Lancet*. 1971; i: 296–297.

153 Lopez A, Hodges RE, Krehl WA. Some interesting relationships between dietary carbohydrates and serum cholesterol. *Am J Clin Nutr* 1966; **18**: 149–153.

154 Keys A. Sucrose in the diet and coronary heart disease. *Atherosclerosis* 1971; **14**: 193–202.

155 Yudkin J, Roddy J. Levels of dietary sucrose in patients with occlusive atherosclerotic disease. *Lancet* 1964; ii: 6–8.

156 Yudkin J, Morland J. Sugar intake and myocardial infarction. *Am J Clin Nutr* 1967; **20**: 503–506.

157 McGandy RB, Hegsted DM, Stare FJ. Dietary fats, carbohydrates and atherosclerotic vascular disease. *N Engl J Med* 1967; **277**: 186–192, 241–247.

158 Walker ARP. Sugar intake and coronary heart disease. *Atherosclerosis* 1971; **14**: 137–152.

159 Grande F. Sugars in cardiovascular disease. In: Sipple HL, McNutt KW, eds. *Sugars in nutrition*. New York: Academic Press, 1974; 401–437.

160 Food and Agriculture Organization and World Health Organization. Joint FAO/WHO Meeting on Carbohydrates in Human Nutrition. *Carbohydrates in human nutrition*. Rome: Food and Agriculture Organization, 1980. (Food and nutrition paper; 15).

161 Finnish Nutrition Committee. *Report on nutrition and public health*. Helsinki: Office of International Affairs, 1981.

162 American Medical Association, International Life Sciences Institute, Nutrition Foundation. Diet and behaviour: a multi-disciplinary evaluation. *Nutrition Reviews* 1986; **44**: supp: 1–254.

163 Schauss AG. *Crime and delinquency*. Berkely: Parker House, 1980.

164 Langseth L, Dowd J. Glucose tolerance and hyperkinesis. *Food Cosmet Toxicol* 1978; **16**: 129–133.

165 Rapp DJ. Does diet affect hyperactivity? *J Learning Disabilities* 1978; **11**: 383–389.

166 Rosenthal NE, Sack DA, Gillin JC, *et al*. Seasonal affective disorder: a description of the syndrome and preliminary findings with light therapy. *Arch Gen Psychiatry* 1984; **41**: 72–80.

167 O'Rourke D, Courtman J, Brelezinski A, Abou-Nader T, Marchant P, Wurtman RJ. Treatment of seasonal affective disorder with d-fenfluramine. *Ann NY Acad Sci* 1987; **449**: 329–330.

168 Tatzer E, Schubert MT, Timischl W, Simbruner G. Discrimination of taste and preference for sweet in premature babies. *Early Hum Dev* 1985; **12**: 23–30.

169 Beauchamp GK, Moran M. Dietary experience and sweet taste preference in human infants. *Appetite* 1982; **3**: 139–152.

170 Burt JV, Hertzler AA. Parental influence on the child's food preference. *J Nutr Educ* 1978; **10**: 127–128.

171 Birch LL. The relation between children's food preferences and those of their parents. *J Nutr Educ* 1980; **12**: 14–18.

172 Pliner P, Pelchat ML. Similarities in food preferences between children and their siblings and parents. *Appetite* 1986; **7**: 333–342.

173 Rome Group for the Epidemiology and Prevention of Cholelithiasis (GREPCO). Prevalence of gallstone disease in an Italian adult female population. *Am J Epidemiol* 1984; **119**: 796–805.

174 Rome Group for the Epidemiology and Prevention of Cholelithiasis (GREPCO). The epidemiology of gallstone disease in Rome. Part I. Prevalence data in men. *Hepatology* 1988; **8**: 904–906.

175 Jørgensen T. Prevalence of gallstones in a Danish population. *Am J Epidemiol* 1987; **126**: 912–921.

176 Heaton K. Gallstones. In: Trowell HC, Burkitt DP, eds. *Western diseases: their emergence and prevention*. London: Edward Arnold, 1981; 47–59.

177 Scragg RKR, McMichael AJ, Baghurst PA. Diet, alcohol and relative weight in gall stone disease: a case-control study. *Br Med J* 1984; **288**: 1113–1119.

178 Alessandrini A, Fuco MA, Gatti E, Ross PA. Dietary fibre and cholesterol gallstones: a case control study. *It J Gastroent* 1982; **14**: 156–158.

179 Attili AF, Rome Group for the Epidemiology and Prevention of Cholelithiasis (GREPCO). Dietary habits and cholelithiasis in epidemiology and prevention of gallstones disease. In: Capocaccia L, Ricci G, Angelico F, Angelico M, Attili A, eds. *Epidemiology and prevention of gallstone disease*. Lancaster: MTP Press, 1984, 175–181.

180 Attili AF, Rome Group for the Epidemiology and Prevention of Cholelithiasis (GREPCO). Diet and gallstones: result of an epidemiologic study performed in male civil servants. In: Barbara L, Bianchi Porro G, Cheli R, Lipkin M, eds. *Nutrition in gastrointestinal disease*. New York: Raven Press, 1987; 225–231.

181 Pixley F, Mann J. Dietary factors in the aetiology of gall stones: a case control study. *Gut* 1988; **29**: 1511–1515.

182 Williams CN, Scullion SM, McCarthy SC. A diet containing highly refined carbohydrate will adversely change bile lipid composition to that seen in cholesterol gallstone disease. *Annals of the Royal College of Physicians and Surgeons of Canada* 1979; **12**: 44.

183 Hood K, Gleeson D, Ruppin D, Dowling RH. Can gallstone recurrence be prevented? The British/Belgian post-dissolution trial. *Gastroenterology* 1988; **94**: A548.

184 Katschinski B, Logan RFA, Edmond M, Langman MJS. Smoking and sugar intake are separate but interactive risk factors in Crohn's disease. *Gut* 1988; **29**: 1202–1206.

185 Heaton KW. Dietary sugar and Crohn's disease. *Can J Gastroent* 1988; **2**: 41–44.

186 Hollander D, Vadheim CM, Brettholz E, Petersen GM, Delahunty T, Rotter JI. Increased intestinal permeability in patients with Crohn's disease and their relatives: a possible etiologic factor. *Ann Intern Med* 1986; **105**: 883–885.

187 Doll R, Peto R. The causes of cancer: quantitative estimates of avoidable risks of cancer in the United States today. *JNCI* 1981; **66**: 1193–1308.

188 Armstrong B, Doll R. Environmental factors and cancer incidence and mortality in different countries, with special reference to dietary practices. *Int J Cancer* 1975; **15**: 617–631.

189 Bristol JB, Emmett PM, Heaton KW, Williamson RCN. Sugar, fat, and the risk of colorectal cancer. *Br Med J* 1985; **291**: 1467–1470.

190 Lyon JL, Mahoney AW, West DW, *et al*. Energy intake: its relationship to colon cancer risk. *JNCI* 1987; **78**: 853–861.

54

191 Potter JD, McMichael AJ. Diet and cancer of the colon and rectum: a case-control study. *JNCI* 1986; **76**: 557–569.

192 Jain M, Cook GM, Davis FG, Grace MG, Howe GR, Miller AB. A case-control study of diet and colo-rectal cancer. *Int J Cancer* 1980; **26**: 757–768.

193 Macquart-Moulin G, Durbec JP, Cornée J, Berthezène P, Southgate DAT. Alimentation et cancer recto-colique. *Gastroenterol Clin Biol* 1983; **7**: 277–286.

194 Berta JL, Coste T, Rautureau J, Guilloud-Bataille M, Péquignot G. Alimentation et cancers recto-coliques: resultats d'une étude 'cas-témoin'. *Gastroenterol Clin Biol* 1985; **9**: 348–353.

195 Lew EA, Garfinkel L. Variations in mortality by weight among 750,000 men and women. *J Chron Dis* 1979; **32**: 563–576.

196 Buell P. Changing incidence of breast cancer in Japanese-American women. *JNCI* 1973; **51**: 1479–1483.

197 Seely S, Horrobin DF. Diet and breast cancer: the possible connection with sugar consumption. *Med Hypotheses* 1983; **11**: 319–327.

198 Reddy BS, Cohen LA, McCoy GD, Hill P, Weisburger JH, Wynder EL. Nutrition and its relation to cancer. *Adv Cancer Res* 1980; **32**: 237–345.

199 Anderson DA. Environmental factors in the aetiology of urolithiasis. In: Cifuentes Delatte L, Rapado A, Hodgkinson A, eds. *Urinary calculi: recent advances in aetiology, stone structure and treatment: proceedings of the International Symposium on Renal Stone Research, Madrid, 1972.* Basel: Karger, 1973; 133–140.

200 Blacklock NJ. Epidemiology of urolithiasis. In: Chisholm GD, Williams DI, eds. *Scientific foundations of urology.* 2nd ed. London: Heinemann Medical, 1982; 251–259.

201 Inada T, Miyazaki S, Omori T, Nihira H, Hino T. Statistical study on urolithiasis in Japan. *Urol Int* 1958; **7**: 150–165.

202 Bulusu L, Hodgkinson A, Nordin BEC, Peacock M. Urinary excretion of calcium and creatinine in relation to age and body weight in normal subjects and patients with renal calculus. *Clin Sci* 1970; **38**: 601–612.

203 Lavan JN, Neale FC, Posen S. Urinary calculi: clinical, biochemical and radiological studies in 619 patients. *Med J Aust* 1971; **2**: 1049–1061.

204 Lemann J, Piering WF, Lennon EJ. Possible role of carbohydrate-induced calciuria in calcium oxalate kidney-stone formation. *N Engl J Med* 1969; **280**: 232–237.

205 Scholz D, Schwille PO. Response of gastrointestinal hormones and intestinal calcium absorption during an oral carbohydrate meal. In: Smith LH, Robertson WG, Finlayson B, eds. *Urolithiasis: clinical and basic research.* New York: Plenum, 1981; 195–800.

206 Rao PN, Gordon C, Davies D, Blacklock NJ. Are stone formers maladapted to refined carbohydrates? *Br J Urol* 1982; **54**: 575–577.

207 Li MK, Kavanagh JP, Prendiville V, Buxton A, Moss DG, Blacklock NJ. Does sucrose damage kidneys? *Br J Urol* 1986; **58**: 353–357.

208 Ferguson A, MacDonald DM, Brydon WG. Prevalence of lactase deficiency in British adults. *Gut* 1984; **25**: 163–167.

209 Ministry of Health. *A pilot survey of the nutrition of young children in 1963.* London: HMSO, 1968. (Reports on public health and medical subjects; no 118).

55

[210] Committee on Medical Aspects of Food Policy. *A nutrition survey of pre-school children 1967–1968*. London: HMSO, 1975. (Reports on health and social subjects; no 10).

[211] Paul AA, Black AE, Evans J, Cole TJ, Whitehead RG. Breastmilk intake and growth in infants from two to ten months. *J Hum Nutr Dietet* 1988; **1**: 437–450.

[212] Paul AA. (Personal communication).

[213] Nelson M, Black AE, Morris JA, Cole TJ. Between and within-subject variation in nutrient intake from infancy to old age: estimating the number of days required to rank dietary intake with required precision. *Am J Clin Nutr* 1989; **50**: 156–167.

[214] Cook J, Altman DG, Moore DMC, Topp SG, Holland WW. A survey of the nutritional status of school children: relation between nutrient intake and socio-economic factors. *Br J Prev Soc Med* 1973; **27**: 91–99.

[215] Darke SJ, Disselduff MM. A nutrition study of primary schoolchildren aged 10–11 years in Bristol, Croydon and Sheffield made in the first three months of 1971. In: Committee on Medical Aspects of Food Policy. *Second report by the sub-committee on nutritional surveillance*. London: HMSO, 1981; 111–130. (Reports on health and social subjects; no 21).

[216] Hackett AF, Rugg-Gunn AJ, Appleton DR, Eastoe JE, Jenkins GN. A 2-year longitudinal nutritional survey of 405 Northumberland children initially aged 11.5 years. *Br J Nutr* 1984; **51**: 67–75.

[217] Rugg-Gunn AJ, Hackett AF, Appleton DR, Moynihan PJ. The dietary intake of added and natural sugars in 405 English adolescents. *Hum Nutr Appl Nutr* 1986; **40A**: 115–124.

[218] Nelson M, Morris J, Barker DJP, Simonds S. A case-control study of acute appendicitis and diet in children. *J Epidemiol Community Health* 1986; **40**: 316–318.

[219] Cole-Hamilton I, Gunner K, Leverkus C, Starr J. A study among dietitians and adult members of their households of the practicalities and implications of following proposed dietary guidelines for the UK. *Hum Nutr App Nutr* 1986; **40A**: 365–389.

[220] Committee on Medical Aspects of Food Policy. *Draft report by the Department of Health and Social Security on a survey of the diets of women in the 6th–7th month of pregnancy, carried out in 1967–68*. 1969 (Unpublished).

[221] Bingham S, McNeil NI, Cummings JH. The diet of individuals: a study of a randomly-chosen cross section of British adults in a Cambridgeshire village. *Br J Nutr* 1981; **45**: 23–35.

[222] Barber SA, Bull NL, Cameron AM. A dietary survey of an isolated population in the UK: the islanders of Orkney. *Hum Nutr App Nutr* 1986; **40A**: 462–469.

[223] Fehily AM, Phillips KM, Sweetnam PM. A weighed dietary survey of men in Caerphilly, South Wales. *Hum Nutr Appl Nutr* 1984; **38A**: 270–276.

[224] Fehily AM, Bird G. The dietary intakes of women in Caerphilly, South Wales: a weighed and a photographic method compared. *Hum Nutr Appl Nutr* 1986; **40A**: 300–307.

[225] Thomson M, Fulton N, Wood DA, *et al*. A comparison of the nutrient intake of some Scotsmen with dietary recommendations. *Hum Nutr Appl Nutr* 1985; **39A**: 443–455.

[226] Black AE, Wiles SJ, Paul AA. The nutrient intakes of pregnant and lactating mothers of good socio-economic status in Cambridge, UK: some implications for recommended daily allowances of minor nutrients. *Br J Nutr* 1986; **56**: 59–72.

227 Schofield C, Wheeler E, Stewart J. The diets of pregnant and post-pregnant women of different social groups in London and Edinburgh: energy, protein, fat and fibre. *Br J Nutr* 1987; **58**: 369–381.

228 Gibney MJ, Moloney N, Shelley E. The Kilkenny Health Project: food and nutrient intakes in randomly selected healthy adults. *Br J Nutr* 1989; **61**: 129–137.

229 Cade JE, Barker DJP, Margetts BM, Morris JA. Diet and inequalities in health in three English towns. *Br Med J* 1988; **296**: 1359–1362.

230 Department of Health and Social Security. *A nutrition survey of the elderly: report by the Panel on Nutrition of the Elderly*. London: HMSO, 1972. (Reports on health and social subjects; no 3).

231 Davies L. *Three score years ... and then? A study of the nutrition and wellbeing of elderly people at home*. London: Heinemann Medical, 1981.

232 Committee on Medical Aspects of Food Policy. *Nutrition and health in old age: the cross-sectional analysis of the findings of a survey made in 1972/3 of elderly people who had been studied in 1967/8: report*. London: HMSO, 1979. (Reports on health and social subjects; no 16).

233 Ministry of Agriculture, Fisheries and Food, Department of Health and Social Security, Welsh Office. *The Food Labelling Regulations 1984*. London: HMSO, 1984. (Statutory Instrument 1984; no 1305).

234 Livesey G, Elia M. Estimation of energy expenditure, net carbohydrate utilization, and net fat oxidation and synthesis by indirect calorimetry: evaluation of errors with special reference to the detailed composition of fuels. *Am J Clin Nutr* 1988; **47**: 608–628.

235 McCance RA, Widdowson EM. *The composition of foods*. 3rd ed. London: HMSO, 1960. (Medical Research Council special report; no 297).

236 Wiles SJ, Nettleton PA, Black AE, Paul AA. The nutrient composition of some cooked dishes eaten in Britain: a supplementary food composition table. *J Hum Nutr* 1980; **34**: 189–223.

237 Black AE, Ravenscroft C, Paul AA. Footnotes to food tables. 1. Differences in nutrient intakes of dietitians as calculated from the DHSS food tables and the fourth edition of *McCance and Widdowson's 'The composition of foods'*. *Hum Nutr Appl Nutr* 1985; **39A**: 9–18.

List of Tables

Table 1   *Mono and disaccharides in foods*

Sucrose

— The following foods normally contain more than 10g sucrose per 100g: drinking chocolate powder, chocolate, condensed milk, sweetened fruit drinks, cakes, biscuits, sugar coated breakfast cereals, sugar confectionery, sweetened alcoholic beverages, preserves, many puddings, ice-cream and ripe bananas.

— Small amounts are added to sauces, many yogurts and other milk desserts, fruit products, processed vegetables and soups.

— Small amounts also occur naturally in cereal grains and flours, fruit and vegetables.

Glucose

— Present in honey, sugar confectionery, preserves, some alcoholic beverages, breakfast cereals, some cakes, sweet biscuits, soft drinks (except low calorie soft drinks), fruit and fruit juices, sauces, soups, sweetened yogurts, ice-cream and vegetables.

— Trace amounts are present in cereal grains and flours.

Fructose

— Mainly present in honey, and in fruit and products containing fruit eg fruit cakes, mueslis, fruit juices, yogurts.

— Small amounts are also present in some alcoholic beverages, soft drinks (not low calorie soft drinks) most vegetables and soups.

— Fructose is added as a sweetener to some diabetic products.

Lactose

— Mainly present in milk (including human milk) and milk products, and also occurs in processed items in which milk, cream, skimmed milk powder or whey is an ingredient eg various mueslis, milk chocolate, instant potato, cream cakes and buns, some puddings, pastries, biscuits and creamed soups.

Maltose

— Present in foods made with glucose syrups eg sugar confectionery items and some infant formulas.

— Small amounts are also present in some biscuits, breakfast cereals.

Foods may contain a number of other sugars including arabinose and xylose (eg in white wine, beer), galactose (fermented milk products), mannose

Table 1   (continued)

(fruit), fucose (human milk and bran), rhamnose (wheat bran), raffinose
(some vegetables), stachyose (beans other than green beans) and verbascose
(oat bran, and legumes). Rarer sugars may also be found in specific foods eg
mannoheptulose in avocado pear, mycose in mushrooms and melezitose and
erlose in honey. Maltotroise and other higher polymers of glucose are also
found in foods made with glucose syrups (maltodextrins) including sugar
confectionery and some infant formulas.

Table 2 *Contribution of food groups to intakes of individual sugars* from the National Food Survey 1987[10] (g/person/day)*

	Glucose	Fructose	Sucrose	Maltose	Lactose	Other
Liquid whole milk	0	0	0	0	11.0	0
Other milk & cream	0.2	0.1	0.8	tr	4.5	0.2
Cheese	0	0	0	0	tr	0
Carcase meat	0	0	0	0	tr	0
All other meat & meat products	0.1	tr	0.1	0.2	tr	tr
Fish & fish products	0	tr	tr	tr	0.1	0
Eggs	0	0	0	0	0	0
Fats	tr	0	0.1	tr	0.2	0.2
Sugar & preserves	2.1	1.4	33.1	0.5	0	0
Potatoes	0.4	0.3	0.6	0	0	0
Fresh green vegetables	0.3	0.3	0.2	0	0	0
Other fresh vegetables	0.8	0.7	0.9	0	0	0.2
Processed vegetables	0.3	0.2	1.7	0	tr	tr
Fresh fruit	1.6	2.8	2.4	0	0	0
Other fruit & fruit products	2.7	2.7	2.8	0.2	0	0
Bread	2.4	0.1	0.6	0.1	tr	0
Flour	0.1	0.1	0.1	tr	0	0
Cakes and biscuits	0.7	0.5	8.2	0.2	0.3	0
Other cereals	0.5	0.4	2.6	0.4	0.3	0
Beverages	tr	0	0.5	0.2	tr	0.1
Miscellaneous	1.0	0.8	2.5	0.1	0.4	tr
TOTAL, ALL FOODS	13.2	10.4	57.0	1.9	16.9	0.8

* Excludes confectionery, alcoholic and soft drinks.

Table 3 *Sucrose, honey and glucose syrups and lactose available for human consumption in the UK*[15-18]

Year	Sucrose g/day A	Honey plus glucose** g/day B	g/day A+B	Lactose g/day	Energy kcal/day	Energy from sucrose as per cent of total energy from food*	Energy from sucrose, honey & glucose as per cent of total
Pre-War	120	6.6	126.6		3050	15.5	16.3
1940	89.4	6.6	96.0		2890	12.2	13.0
1941	81.9	3.7	85.6		2900	11.1	11.6
1942	82.8	3.1	85.9		2930	11.2	11.6
1943	82.6	2.9	85.5		2920	11.1	11.5
1944	87.7	3.2	90.9		3060	11.3	11.7
1945	83.1	3.4	86.5		3010	10.9	11.3
1946	95.1	3.4	98.5		2940	12.7	13.2
1947	100.3	3.9	104.2		2940	13.4	13.9
1948	102.2	3.8	106.0		3000	13.4	13.9
1949	112.6	5.1	117.7		3120	14.2	14.8
1950	103.5	4.5	108.0		3120	13.1	13.6
1951	114.7	5.0	119.7		3080	14.7	15.3
1952	108.7	4.8	113.5		3030	14.1	14.7
1953	119.3	7.1	126.4		3100	15.1	16.0
1954	128.1	7.1	135.2		3190	15.8	16.6
1955	131.4	7.6	139.0		3170	16.3	17.2
1956	132.5	7.4	139.9		3170	16.5	17.3
1957	135.2	7.8	143.0		3180	16.7	17.7
1958	139.7	7.8	147.5		3180	17.3	18.2
1959	134.3	7.6	141.9		3130	16.9	17.8
1960	134.6	8.1	142.7		3140	16.9	17.8
1961	137.1	8.3	145.4		3150	17.1	18.1
1962	134.0	8.3	142.3		3170	16.6	17.6
1963	134.6	8.9	143.5		3180	16.7	17.7
1964	129.3	9.2	138.5		3160	16.1	17.2

Table 3 (Continued)

Year	Sucrose g/day A	Honey plus glucose** g/day B	g/day A+B	Lactose g/day	Energy kcal/day	Energy from sucrose as per cent of total energy from food*	Energy from sucrose, honey & glucose as per cent of total
1965	130.1	10.3	140.4		3140	16.3	17.5
1966	131.5	10.6	142.1		3160	16.4	17.6
1967	128.7	11.1	139.8		3080	16.5	17.8
1968	126.7	11.8	138.5		3090	16.1	17.5
1969	128.1	12.8	140.9		3110	16.2	17.8
1970	126.8	13.2	140.0		3110	16.1	17.6
1971	124.1	13.5	137.6		3080	15.9	17.5
1972	125.4	14.2	139.6		3060	16.1	17.9
1973	123.3	15.6	138.9		3040	16.0	17.9
1974	125.5	16.7	142.2	22	2960	16.7	18.8
1975	98.6	19.2	117.8	22	2917	13.3	15.8
1976	112.3	20.8	133.1	21	3003	14.7	17.3
1977	112.1	19.5	131.6	23	3061	14.4	16.8
1978	111.5	21.4	132.9	23	2988	14.7	17.4
1979	108.5	20.0	128.5	23	2980	14.3	16.9
1980	101.1	17.5	118.6	22.1	2851	14.0	16.3
1981	100.5	16.2	116.7	22.9	2863	13.8	15.9
1982	106.8	16.2	123.0	22.5	2883	14.6	16.7
1983	102.5	16.2	118.7	23.2	2872	14.1	16.2
1984	103.6	17.2	120.8	24.5	2891	14.1	16.3
1985	101.6	16.7	118.3	24.4	2919	13.7	15.9
1986	101.9	17.3	119.2	21.3	2970	13.5	15.7
1987	103.8	16.4	120.2	22.7	2992	13.7	15.7

* Excludes energy from alcoholic drinks.

** Excluding glucose and other sugars in fruit and vegetables.

63

Table 4 *Sugars intake by pre-school children Mean (s.d.)*

Author, Location, date	Ages	Sample number gender	Intake per day				Percent energy	
			Energy		Total sugars g	Non-milk extrinsic sugars g	Total sugars %	Non-milk extrinsic sugars %
			MJ	kcal				
Ministry of Health,[209] England, 1963	1–2y	88 M&F	4.69 (1.18)	1117 (281)	—	43 (18.8)	—	14.4
	2–3y	92 M&F	5.67 (1.53)	1349 (364)	—	57 (28.8)	—	15.8
	3–4y	84 M&F	5.63 (1.08)	1341 (256)	—	60 (18.3)	—	16.8
	4–5y	79 M&F	6.49 (1.45)	1545 (346)	—	68 (24.7)	—	16.5
DHSS,[210] England, Wales & Scotland, 1967/68	6–18m	201 M&F	4.41 (1.06)	1050 (252)	—	48.0 (22.0)	—	18.3
	1.5–2.5y	394 M&F	5.30 (1.34)	1262 (320)	—	56.8 (23.0)	—	18.0
	2.5–3.5y	407 M&F	5.88 (1.51)	1401 (360)	—	64.7 (24.6)	—	18.5
	3.5–4.5y	319 M&F	6.16 (1.59)	1468 (378)	—	69.4 (23.6)	—	18.9
Paul et al[211,212] and unpublished Cambridge, 1978–82 (Longitudinal study)	15m	36 M&F	3.93 (0.92)	936 (219)	64 (25)	31 (20)	25.7 (8.8)	12.4 (8.1)
	18m	34 M&F	3.99 (1.07)	948 (255)	72 (25)	37 (23)	28.5 (7.6)	14.4 (8.3)
	24m	30 M&F	4.35 (0.75)	1034 (180)	79 (19)	44 (19)	29.0 (7.5)	16.4 (7.9)
	36m	39 M&F	4.87 (0.65)	1159 (154)	86 (24)	50 (24)	27.9 (7.3)	16.1 (7.8)
Nelson,[25,213] Cambridge, 1977–79	1–4y	35 M	6.19 (1.47)	1474 (350)	102 (34)	—	26.0	—
		34 F	5.70 (1.35)	1357 (321)	101 (31)	—	27.8	—

Table 5 *Sugars intake by schoolchildren Mean (s.d.)*

Author, Location, date	Ages	Sample number gender	Intake per day					Percent energy	
			Energy		Total sugars	Non-milk extrinsic sugars		Total sugars	Non-milk extrinsic sugars
			MJ	kcal	g	g		%	%
Cook et al [214] Kent, 1968/70	8–15y	355 M	10.68	2543	–	113.2		–	16.7
		341 F	8.50	2024	–	90.4		–	16.7
	8–11y	352 M+F	8.99	2141	–	97.4		–	17.1
	12–15y	344 M+F	10.25	2441	–	107.8		–	16.4
Darke and Disselduff, [215] Bristol, Croydon & Sheffield, 1971	10–11y	163 M	9.08 (1.63)	2169 (390)	–	95		–	16.4
		158 F	8.02 (1.56)	1916 (372)	–	85		–	16.7
Nelson [25,213] Cambridge 1977/79	5–10y	56 M	7.86 (1.77)	1871 (420)	118 (38)	–		23.7	–
	11–17y	45 M	10.33 (2.19)	2460 (521)	139 (43)	–		21.2	–
	5–10y	53 F	7.14 (1.52)	1700 (362)	112 (35)	–		24.7	–
	11–17y	35 F	8.71 (1.89)	2074 (450)	118 (39)	–		21.3	–
Hackett et al [216] Rugg Gunn et al [217] Northumberland 1979/81	11.5– 13.5y	184 M	9.4 (1.4)	2238 (333)	123 (27)	84.3 (21.3)		20.9	14.3
		191 F	8.5 (1.4)	2023 (333)	114 (30)	77.6 (22.6)		21.5	14.6
Nelson et al [218,219] Southampton 1982	13–15y	63 M	10.29 (2.33)	2450 (555)	133 (43)	–		20.4	
	13–15y	34 F	8.03 (1.94)	1912 (462)	97 (38)	–		19.0	

Table 6 *Sugars intake by adults Mean (s.d.)*

Author, Location, date	Ages	Sample number gender	Intake per day				Percent energy	
			Energy		Total sugars	Non-milk extrinsic sugars	Total sugars	Non-milk extrinsic sugars
			MJ	kcal	g	g	%	%
COMA,[220] Throughout UK 1967–68	Pregnant 2nd trimester	435 F	9.04	2152		70		12.2
Bingham et al [221] and unpublished Cambridgeshire 1977	20–39y	13 M	10.23 (1.80)	2435 (428)	122 (46)	83.8 (38.8)	18.9 (5.7)	12.8 (5.3)
	40–59y	12 M	9.86 (3.03)	2348 (721)	129 (63)	87.2 (46.5)	21.2 (7.5)	14.1 (7.0)
	20–39y	10 F	9.17 (1.90)	2183 (452)	118 (37)	72.1 (29.4)	21.5 (6.0)	12.8 (6.0)
	40–59y	14 F	8.34 (1.84)	1986 (438)	108 (40)	60.4 (33.9)	20.4 (5.0)	10.7 (5.3)
Smithells et al [34] and unpublished Leeds, 1969–76	Pregnant 1st trimester	195 F	7.83 (1.82)	1864 (434)	101 (41)	61 (34)	20.1 (5.9)	12.1 (5.5)
Black et al [31] and unpublished Throughout UK 1977	20–59y Dieticians	42 F	7.67 (1.63)	1827 (389)	98 (29)	37 (19)	20.4 (5.4)	7.3 (2.7)
Nelson,[24,25] and unpublished Cambridge 1977–79	18–57y	105 M	11.68 (2.67)	2786 (637)	151 (63)	107 (58)	20.1 (6.5)	14.2 (6.5)
	18–53y	112 F	8.16 (1.87)	1946 (445)	103 (43)	62 (38)	19.5 (6.5)	11.7 (6.5)
Barber et al [2,222] Orkney, 1980	18–82y	40 M	12.97 (2.50)	3098 (593)	131*	—	16*	—
	19–75y	78 F	8.6 (1.70)	2053 (413)	83*	—	17*	—
Fehily et al [223,224] and unpublished Caerphilly, S Wales 1980–83	45–59y	665 M	10.00 (2.5)	2395 (585)	109 (56)	—	17.1	—
	40–59y	49 F	6.68 (1.5)	1600 (366)	67 (35)	—	15.7	—

Table 6 (Continued)

Author, Location, date	Ages	Sample number gender	Intake per day				Percent energy	
			Energy		Total sugars	Non-milk extrinsic sugars	Total sugars	Non-milk extrinsic sugars
			MJ	kcal	g	g	%	%
Thomson et al [2,225] Fifeshire, 1980–82	45–54y	164 M	11.3 (2.1)	2700 (510)	141	–	19.5	–
Black et al [226] and unpublished, Cambridge 1978–1980 (Longitudinal Study)	Pregnant	63 F	8.69 (1.39)	2072 (331)	106 (28)	49 (19)	19.2 (3.5)	8.9 (3.0)
	Lactating	47 F	10.04 (1.77)	2393 (422)	125 (33)	56 (21)	19.4 (3.2)	8.7 (2.8)
	Non pregnant Non lactating	56 F	7.93 (1.64)	1892 (390)	90 (35)	45(28)	17.6 (4.9)	8.8 (4.9)
Schofield et al [2,227] and unpublished Edinburgh and London, 1983–85	18–35y Pregnant	260 F	8.7	2080	90*		16.0*	–
Cole-Hamilton et al [219] Throughout UK 1984	Dietitians and their families	142 M	11.25 (1.76)	2679 (419)	125 (36)	112 (31)	17.5	8.3 (3.3)
		209 F	7.99 (1.54)	1902 (367)	98 (28)	43 (21)	19.3	8.9 (3.9)
Gibney et al [229] Kilkenny, 1985	35–44y	30 M	12.5 (2.6)	2976 (619)	164	–	20.7	–
		30 F	8.4 (2.2)	2000 (523)	102	–	19.1	–
Gibney and Lee [23] Dublin, 1987	Adults	42 M	13.1 (3.0)	3119 (714)	209	–	25.1	–
		55 F	8.5 (2.8)	2023 (666)	153	–	28.4	–
Doyle et al [32] and unpublished London, 1988	Pregnant 1st Trimester	419 F	8.4 (1.8)	2011 (426)	102 (35)	55.6 (28)	18.9	10.2

Table 6 (Continued)

| Author, Location, date | Ages | Sample number gender | Intake per day | | | | Percent energy | |
| | | | Energy | | Total sugars | Non-milk extrinsic sugars | Total sugars | Non-milk extrinsic sugars |
			MJ	kcal	g	g	%	%
Cade et al [229] unpublished Ipswich, Stoke and Wakefield, 1987	35–54y	1115 M	10.95 (3.58)	2607 (852)	119.7 (60)	—	18.6 (6.7)	—
		1225 F	7.11 (2.57)	1693 (612)	78.2 (46)	—	18.6 (7.0)	—

* excluding lactose

Table 7 *Sugars consumption by some elderly groups Mean (s.d.)*

Author, Location, date	Ages	Sample number gender	Intake per day				Percent energy	
			Energy		Total sugars	Non-milk extrinsic sugars	Total sugars	Non-milk extrinsic sugars
			MJ	kcal	g	g	%	%
DHSS,[230] 6 areas of England and Scotland, 1967–68	over 65y	827 M&F	8.2	1962	—	63	—	12–14
Davies,[231] Portsmouth, 1970	65–74y	10 M	9.0 (6.1–12.5)	2160 (1450–3000)	—	105 (52–198)	—	18.2
	75+y	16 M	9.0 (6.5–11.1)	2150 (1550–2660)	—	87 (13–147)	—	15.2
Recipients of meals on-wheels	65–74y	24 F	6.7 (4.2–9.8)	1600 (1000–2340)	—	53 (6–112)	—	12.4
	75+y	50 F	7.3 (5.1–11.0)	1750 (1210–2640)	—	66 (5–160)	—	14.1
DHSS,[232] 6 areas of England and Scotland, 1972–73	70–80y	111 M	9.3 (2.2)	2217 (522)	—	71.6 (35.7)	—	12.7 (5.3)
	Over 80y	58 M	8.5 (2.1)	2024 (498)	—	66.0 (33.0)	—	13.2 (6.8)
	70–80y	125 F	7.0 (1.7)	1679 (416)	—	48.8 (27.0)	—	11.5 (5.5)
	Over 80y	71 F	6.5 (1.5)	1559 (358)	—	48.5 (28.3)	—	12.2 (6.0)
Bingham et al [221] Cambridgeshire, 1977	60–79y	7 M	9.90 (2.57)	2357 (612)	156 (66)	111.0 (62.2)	25.2 (5.1)	16.8 (5.3)
		7 F	6.42 (1.92)	1529 (457)	61 (16)	27.2 (13.6)	16.5 (4.9)	6.6 (3.0)

Table 8 *The contribution of various food groups to the sugars content of the diet*

	Northumberland schoolchildren 1986[217] (n = 405, both sexes)		Cambridge adults*			
			Women (n = 112)		Men (n = 105)	
	Sugars		Sugars		Sugars	
Groups of foods	Non-milk extrinsic g/d	Intrinsic plus milk sugars g/d	Non-milk extrinsic g/d	Intrinsic plus milk sugars g/d	Non-milk extrinsic g/d	Intrinsic plus milk sugars g/d
Confectionery	23.0	1.3	4.2	0.2	3.3	0.2
Table sugar	19.6	—	27.3	—	63.4	—
Soft drinks and fruit juices	13.6	2.4	4.7	1.8	3.8	1.3
Biscuits and cakes	10.1	2.9	9.7	3.5	11.2	5.1
Sweet puddings, including fruit pies	7.2	5.5	5.0	1.9	6.3	2.7
Syrups and preserves	2.8	1.5	3.8	1.6	4.4	2.0
Breakfast cereals	2.3	0.5	0.7	0.7	0.8	0.8
Milk, butter, cheese and yogurt	0	11.8	2.4	17.4	2.4	17.7
Fruit	0	5.5	1.3	6.7	1.0	5.3
Rice, pasta, bread	} 2.7	} 5.7	0	1.6	0.1	2.4
Potatoes and vegetables			0.9	3.2	1.2	4.0
Others			2.1	1.7	9.3	1.7
Totals	81.3	37.1	62.1	40.3	107.1	43.2

* data of Nelson and Paul (Unpublished)

Table 9 Nutrient intake of 105 men and 112 women in Cambridge by thirds of the distribution of energy intake

Total intake (per day)	Men				Women			
	Lowest	Middle	Highest	p	Lowest	Middle	Highest	p
Number in third	35	35	35		37	38	37	
Energy, kcal	2168	2673	3448		1475	1944	2416	
range	1443–2418	2427–2933	3003–5042		794–1777	1791–2134	2150–3318	
Protein g	74	85	105	+++	54	66	75	+++
Fat g	94	115	151	+++	69	88	110	+++
Carbohydrate g	254	323	397	+++	163	226	284	+++
Alcohol g	9	12	25	ns	4	5	8	ns
Total sugars g	107	153	188	+++	72	103	134	+++
Non milk extrinsic sugars g	74	107	138	+++	42	61	83	+++
Magnesium mg	266	321	392	+++	188	241	292	+++
Zinc mg	9.2	10.8	13.2	+++	6.9	8.0	9.5	+++
Iron mg	11.1	13.1	16.4	+++	8.5	9.9	12.2	+++
Thiamin mg	1.11	1.30	1.53	+++	0.78	1.04	1.14	+++
Calcium mg	832	1147	1350	+++	667	934	1080	+++
Vitamin C mg	48	59	63	++	42	51	69	++
Intakes/1000 kcal								
Protein g	34.0	31.6	30.5	+++	36.7	33.7	31.0	+++
Fat g	43.5	43.0	43.9	ns	46.5	45.5	45.6	ns
Carbohydrate g	117.3	120.6	115.0	ns	110.2	116.2	117.7	ns
Alcohol g	4.2	4.5	7.1	ns	2.6	2.4	3.2	ns
Total sugars g	49.2	57.3	54.6	ns	48.9	52.7	55.5	ns
Non-milk extrinsic sugars g	34.1	40.0	40.1	ns	28.5	31.4	34.3	ns

Table 9 (Continued)

Total intake (per day)	Men				Women			
	Lowest	Middle	Highest	p	Lowest	Middle	Highest	p
Number in third	35	35	35		37	38	37	
Energy, kcal	2168	2673	3448	+++	1475	1944	2416	+++
range	1443–2418	2427–2933	3003–5042		794–1777	1791–2134	2150–3318	
Magnesium mg	123	120	114	ns	127	124	121	ns
Zinc mg	4.25	4.04	3.83	+	4.67	4.12	3.92	++
Iron mg	5.12	4.89	4.77	ns	5.75	5.09	5.05	ns
Thiamin mg	0.51	0.49	0.44	+	0.53	0.53	0.47	ns
Calcium mg	384	429	392	ns	452	480	447	ns
Vitamin C mg	22	22	18	ns	28	26	29	ns

+++ $p < 0.001$; ++ $p < 0.01$, + $p < 0.05$; ns – not significant (lowest vs highest)
data of Nelson and Paul (unpublished) (see Appendix E)

Table 10 Nutrient intake of 105 men and 112 women in Cambridge according to the proportion of sugar in the diet (expressed as grams of non-milk extrinsic sugars per 1000 kcal)

	Men				Women			
	Lowest	Middle	Highest	p	Lowest	Middle	Highest	p
Number in third	35	35	35		37	38	37	
Non-milk extrinsic sugars g per 1000 kcal	20.4	38.6	55.8	+++	16.2	28.8	49.6	+++
range	9.0–30.6	31.2–43.1	43.9–109.6		5.2–22.3	22.4–36.5	36.9–111.2	
Total intake (per day)								
Energy, kcal	2594	3016	2679	ns	1825	2023	1985	ns
Protein g	89	93	81	ns	67	68	60	+
Fat g	123	127	111	ns	90	93	85	ns
Carbohydrate g	271	358	345	ns	187	229	257	+++
Alcohol g	16	22	8	+++	6	8	3	+
Total sugars g	97	163	190	+++	73	102	135	+++
Non-milk extrinsic sugars g	53	117	149	+++	30	58	99	+++
Magnesium mg	324	367	287	ns	241	251	228	ns
Zinc mg	11.3	11.8	10.2	ns	8.5	8.4	7.4	+
Iron mg	14.0	14.1	12.5	ns	10.6	10.8	9.2	+
Thiamin mg	1.32	1.40	1.22	ns	0.98	1.05	0.92	ns
Calcium mg	1122	1185	1023	ns	906	937	837	ns
Vitamin C mg	55	62	53	ns	54	53	54	ns
Intake/1000 kcal								
Protein g	34.2	31.0	30.3	+++	36.6	33.6	30.1	+++
Fat g	47.3	42.1	41.4	+++	49.3	45.7	42.6	+++
Carbohydrate, g	104.5	118.7	128.6	+++	102.6	113.1	129.2	+++
Alcohol g	6.2	7.2	2.9	ns	3.2	3.9	1.3	ns
Total sugars g	37.3	54.1	70.8	+++	40.0	50.5	68.1	+++

Table 10 (Continued)

	Men				Women			
	Lowest	Middle	Highest	p	Lowest	Middle	Highest	p
Number in third	35	35	35		37	38	37	
Non-milk extrinsic sugars g per 1000 kcal	20.4	38.6	55.8	+++	16.2	28.8	49.6	+++
range	9.0–30.6	31.2–43.1	43.9–109.6		5.2–22.3	22.4–36.5	36.9–111.2	
Magnesium mg	125	122	107	+++	132	124	115	++
Zinc mg	4.40	3.91	3.80	+++	4.66	4.17	3.74	+++
Iron mg	5.40	4.68	4.68	++	5.82	5.33	4.61	+++
Thiamin mg	0.52	0.46	0.46	+	0.54	0.51	0.46	+
Calcium mg	426	393	382	ns	496	463	422	+
Vitamin C mg	22	20	20	ns	30	26	27	ns

+++ p<0.001; ++ p<0.01; + p<0.05; ns – not significant (lowest vs highest)
data of Nelson and Paul (unpublished) (see Appendix E)

Table 11 Nutrient intake according to intake of non-milk extrinsic sugars within three levels of energy intake in Cambridge adults (kcal per day)

		CAMBRIDGE MEN (n=105)								
Energy intake (kcal)		Highest (3003–5042)			Middle (2427–2953)			Lowest (1443–2418)		
Non-milk extrinsic sugars intake (g per 1000 kcal)		Higher 41.1–99.4	p	Lower 19.0–41.0	Higher 41.5–109.6	p	Lower 9.0–41.3	Higher 32.8–84.1	p	Lower 9.6–32.0
number		18		17	18		17	18		17
	RDA [27, 28]									
Nutrient intake										
Energy kcal		3625	ns	3260	2690	ns	2656	2180	ns	2155
Protein g		104	ns	106	83	ns	87	70	ns	78
Fat g		150	ns	152	110	+	120	89	+	100
Total CHO g		448	+++	343	350	++	294	279	+++	228
Total sugars g		231	+++	144	190	+++	115	137	+++	75
Non-milk extrinsic sugars g		180	+++	94	141	+++	71	105	+++	41
Alcohol g		25	ns	25	7	ns	18	7	ns	12
Magnesium mg	350	401	ns	383	307	ns	335	261	ns	270
Zinc mg	15	12.9	ns	13.6	10.3	ns	11.3	8.7	ns	9.8
Iron mg	10	16.5	ns	16.4	12.1	+	14.1	10.8	+++	11.5
Calcium mg	500	1388	ns	1309	1154	ns	1139	820	ns	845
Thiamin mg	1.0–1.3	1.50	ns	1.56	1.30	ns	1.30	1.02	ns	1.20
Vitamin C mg	30	66	ns	59	61	ns	58	42	ns	53
Per cent of energy										
Protein		11.5	+++	13.0	12.3	ns	13.0	12.8	+++	14.5
Fat		37.3	+	42.0	36.9	+	40.7	36.8	+++	41.8
Total carbohydrate		46.3	+++	39.4	48.8	+++	41.5	48.0	+++	39.7
Total sugars		23.9	+++	16.6	26.5	+++	16.3	23.6	+++	13.2
Non-milk extrinsic sugars		18.6	+++	10.8	19.7	+++	10.0	18.0	+++	7.2

Table 11 (Continued)

	RDA[27,28]	CAMBRIDGE WOMEN (n=112)								
Energy intake (kcal)		Highest (2150–3318)			Middle (1791–2134)			Lowest (794–1777)		
Non-milk extrinsic sugars intake (g per 1000 kcal)		Higher	p	Lower	Higher	p	Lower	Higher	p	Lower
		32.8–84.4		10.9–31.8	26.2–71.0		12.0–25.9	23.8–111.1		5.2–19.9
Number		18		19	19		19	18		19
Nutrient intake										
Energy kcal		2507	+	2337	1934	ns	1953	1433	ns	1515
Protein g		72	ns	77	63	+	68	49	+	59
Fat g		110	ns	110	83	+	94	61	++	76
Total CHO g		318	+++	253	243	+++	209	177	++	149
Total sugars g		160	+++	106	119	+++	87	89	++	56
Non-milk extrinsic sugars g		109	+++	52	80	+++	43	65	+++	21
Alcohol g		6	+	11	3	+	7	2	ns	5
Magnesium mg	300	289	ns	247	241	ns	241	166	+	208
Zinc mg	15	9.0	ns	10.0	7.7	ns	8.3	6.2	+	7.6
Iron mg	12	11.6	ns	12.9	9.2	+	10.6	7.4	+	9.5
Calcium mg	500	1080	ns	1079	881	ns	986	591	ns	740
Thiamin mg	0.9	1.10	ns	1.18	1.05	ns	1.02	0.74	ns	0.83
Vitamin C mg	30	74	ns	64	45	+	56	37	ns	46
Per cent of energy										
Protein		11.6	++	13.3	13.0	ns	14.0	13.6	+	15.6
Fat		39.6	+	42.5	38.7	+++	43.2	38.5	+++	44.9
Total carbohydrate		47.5	+++	40.7	47.1	+++	40.1	46.3	+++	36.9
Total sugars		23.9	+++	17.1	23.1	+++	16.7	23.5	+++	13.9
Non-milk extrinsic sugars		16.3	+++	8.5	15.5	+++	8.1	17.0	+++	5.1

+++ p<0.001; ++ p<0.01; + p<0.05; ns—not significant

Data of Nelson and Paul, unpublished (see Appendix E).

Table 12 *Nutrient intake of pregnant women in Leeds according to intake of non-milk extrinsic sugars per 1000 kcal within three levels of energy intake*

Energy intake	Highest			Middle			Lowest		
Non-milk extrinsic sugars intake (g per 1000 kcal)	Higher 43.4	Lower 23.2	p	Higher 43.1	Lower 24.0	p	Higher 42.4	Lower 18.0	p
Range	30.8–105.9	10.7–30.5		32.8–74.9	12.3–32.8		28.4–77.4	3.1–27.0	
Number	32	33		33	33		32	33	
Nutrient intake									
Energy kcal	2314	2362	ns	1880	1913	ns	1421	1390	ns
Protein g	78	87	++	63	70	++	49	58	++
Fat g	100	111	+++	80	89	+++	60	66	ns
Total carbohydrate g	290	265	+	237	219	+++	178	151	++
Total sugars g	154	109	+++	122	88	+++	88	52	+++
Non-milk extrinsic sugars g	102	55	+++	81	46	+++	60	26	+++
Alcohol g	3	3	ns	2	2	ns	2	0	ns
Magnesium mg	258	265	ns	212	219	ns	153	159	ns
Zinc mg	9.4	10.4	+	7.9	8.3	ns	5.6	7.0	++
Iron mg	10.7	11.5	ns	9.2	9.3	ns	6.5	7.7	++
Calcium mg	1115	1150	ns	902	930	ns	619	653	ns
Thiamin mg	1.22	1.32	ns	0.99	1.08	ns	0.75	1.08	+
Vitamin C mg	78	76	ns	58	60	ns	41	41	ns

Table 12 (Continued)

Energy intake	Highest			Middle			Lowest		
	Higher	p	Lower	Higher	p	Lower	Higher	p	Lower
Non-milk extrinsic sugars intake (g per 1000 kcal)	43.4		23.2	43.1		24.0	42.4		18.0
Per cent of energy									
Protein	13.5	+	14.7	13.4	++	14.7	13.7	+++	16.6
Fat	38.9	+++	42.3	38.4	+++	41.7	38.0	+++	42.5
Total carbohydrate	47.1	+++	42.1	47.3	+++	42.9	47.4	+++	40.8
Total sugars	24.9	+++	17.3	24.4	+++	17.2	23.2	+++	14.0
Non-milk extrinsic sugars	16.5	+++	8.7	16.1	+++	9.0	15.9	+++	6.9

+ + + p<0.001; + + p<0.01; + p<0.05; ns – not significant

Data of Smithells *et al*[34] and unpublished (see Appendix E).

Table 13 *Daily intake of nutrients of unemployed families in Dublin*

Nutrient	Men		Women		Quartile of table sugar intake			
					Men		Women	
	Mean	(sd)	Mean	(sd)	Lowest	Highest	Lowest	Highest
number	42		55		10	10	15	12
Intake:								
Energy (MJ)	13.1	(3.0)	8.5	(2.8)	11.7	15.0	7.2	11.6
Protein (g)	100	(25)	64	(18)	91	100	64	69
Fat (g)	128	(33)	81	(24)	127	123	81	83
Carbohydrate (g)	409	(128)	275	(131)	312	552	191	460
Starch (g)	200	(62)	122	(48)	198	190	120	105
Fibre (g)	21.5	(6.4)	13.9	(5.0)	19.6	21.1	13.8	14.1
Iron (mg)	13.5	(3.2)	8.1	(2.3)	13.1	12.8	7.5	8.7
Zinc (mg)	12.9	(3.6)	8.3	(2.5)	12.2	12.6	8.4	8.6
Vitamin C (mg)	60	(21)	45	(18)	57	60	43	49
Retinol (µg)	1507	(1299)	1070	(1032)	1484	1339	1050	1317
Table sugar (g)	95	(99)	73	(100)	0	242	0	231
Body mass index (kg/m^2)	24.5	(3.6)	23.2	(4.3)	25.8	23.9	23.1	23.5

Data of Gibney and Lee[23]

Table 14 *Percentage distribution of Quetelet index by age and sex among British adults*

Body Mass Index	All ages 16-64	16-19	20-24	25-29	30-34	35-39	40-44	45-49	50-54	55-59	60-64
	%	%	%	%	%	%	%	%	%	%	%
Men											
20 or under	10	33	14	9	7	8	3	3	5	7	6
Over 20-25	51	56	64	61	53	51	47	43	44	43	39
Over 25-30	33	9	19	26	34	35	42	44	45	42	44
Over 30-35	5	2	3	3	5	5	7	9	5	7	10
Over 35-40	1	–	–	0	1	1	1	1	0	1	0
Over 40	0	–	–	–	–	0	0	–	–	–	0
Base	4,499	480	516	537	520	453	433	394	417	427	316
Average value	24.3	21.4	23.0	23.8	24.5	24.7	25.3	25.7	25.2	25.2	25.4
Median value	24.5	21.5	22.5	23.5	24.5	24.5	25.3	25.5	25.5	25.5	25.5
Standard error of average	0.05	0.15	0.15	0.13	0.13	0.19	0.15	0.19	0.17	0.17	0.25

Table 14 (Continued)

Body Mass Index	All ages										
	16–64	16–19	20–24	25–29	30–34	35–39	40–44	45–49	50–54	55–59	60–64
	%	%	%	%	%	%	%	%	%	%	%
Women											
20 or under	14	33	23	18	16	11	7	7	9	6	8
Over 20–25	54	53	56	62	57	61	57	54	48	46	41
Over 25–30	24	11	16	14	22	20	28	28	30	34	36
Over 30–35	6	2	4	4	4	6	6	7	10	12	10
Over 35–40	2	0	1	1	0	2	2	2	3	1	4
Over 40	0	0	0	0	0	0	1	1	1	1	1
Base	4,935	497	547	556	559	492	481	413	491	484	398
Average value	23.9	21.8	22.7	22.9	23.4	23.9	24.6	24.9	25.2	25.4	25.7
Median value	23.5	21.5	22.5	21.5	22.5	23.5	23.5	24.5	24.5	24.5	25.5
Standard error of average	0.08	0.14	0.18	0.17	0.15	0.16	0.19	0.19	0.24	0.18	0.25

Data of Knight[124]

81

List of Figures

Figure 1. Supplies of selected sugars since 1850 expressed as grams per head of the population per day

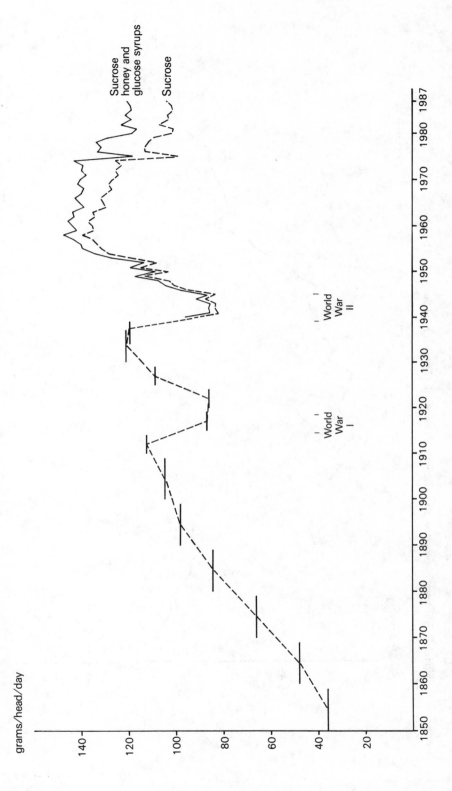

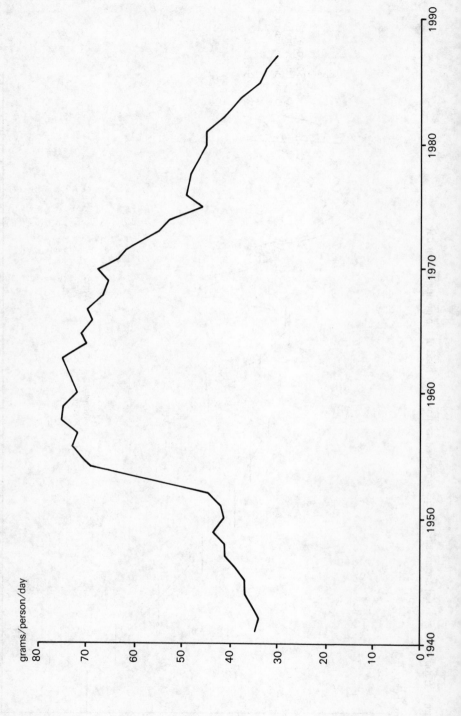

Figure 2. Purchases of packet sugar recorded in Britain by the National Food Survey 1941-1987

grams/person/day

84

Appendices

Appendix A: Affiliations of Members of the Panel

Chairman

Professor H Keen · Unit for Metabolic Medicine,
United Medical and Dental Schools of Guy's
and St Thomas's Hospitals,
Guy's Campus,
University of London.

Members

Miss A E Black · The MRC Dunn Nutrition Unit, Cambridge.

Professor
J V G A Durnin · Institute of Physiology, University of Glasgow.

Professor J S Garrow · Department of Human Nutrition,
Medical College of St Bartholomew's and the
London Hospitals,
University of London.

Dr K W Heaton · University Department of Medicine,
The Royal Infirmary, Bristol.

Professor A A Jackson · Department of Human Nutrition,
School of Biochemical and Physiological
Sciences,
University of Southampton.

Professor J I Mann · Department of Nutrition,
University of Otago, Dunedin,
New Zealand.

Professor D J Naismith · Department of Nutrition,
King's College,
University of London.

Dr E Newsholme · Department of Biochemistry,
University of Oxford.

Professor N W Read · Department of Physiology,
University of Sheffield.

Professor A J Rugg-Gunn	Departments of Child Dental Health and Oral Biology, The Dental School, University of Newcastle Upon Tyne.
Professor T Silverstone	Department of Psychological Medicine, Medical College of St Bartholomew's Hospital, University of London.

Observers

Dr J G Ablett	Department of Health, London.
Dr D H Buss	Ministry of Agriculture, Fisheries and Food, London.
Dr P C Clarke	Department of Health, London.
Mr C Howard	Department of Health, London.

Secretariat

Dr M J Wiseman (Medical)	Department of Health, London.
Mr R W Wenlock (Scientific)	Department of Health, London.
Mr K L G Follin (Administrative)	Department of Health, London.
Mrs N Bateson (Administrative)	Department of Health, London.
Mrs E Lohani (Administrative)	Department of Health, London.
Mr D Roberts (Administrative)	Department of Health, London.

Appendix B: Individuals and Organisations who submitted evidence to the Panel

We wish to record our indebtedness to the following individuals and organisations who have assisted us by contributing evidence and to express our thanks for their help.

Dr D Benton   Department of Psychology,
University College,
Swansea

Dr B Bibby   Eastman Dental Centre,
New York

Billingtons
Edward Billington (Sugar) Ltd

Biscuit, Cake, Chocolate
and Confectionary
Alliance

Janet Cade and others   MRC Environmental Epidemiology Unit,
Southampton

M J Campbell   Department of Medical Statistics and Computing,
University of Southampton

Coronary Prevention Group

Dr A M Cushing   For Action and Information on Sugars

Finn Sugar Xyrofin

Food and Drink Federation

Food Policy Research   University of Bradford
Unit

A D French   British Association for the Study of Community
Dentistry

J R Goodman   The British Paedodontic Society, London

Irish Sugar PLC

Professor W P T James   The Rowett Research Institute, Aberdeen

87

Dr S Kreitzman	University of Cambridge Clinical School
M McClusky	Kenilworth, Warwickshire
M Midda	University of Bristol Dental Hospital, Bristol
Miss J Scott	Community Dietician Representing The Community Nutrition Group of the British Dietetic Association
Professor A Sheiham	Department of Community Dental Health and Dental Practice, School of Medicine, University College Hospital London
Society for the Understanding of Nutrition	
Sugar Bureau	
Tate and Lyle PLC	
Dr A R P Walker	Human Biochemistry Research Unit, South African Institute for Medical Research, Johannesburgh, South Africa,
Dr J T Winkler	King's Fund Institute, London
Professor J Yudkin	Emeritus Professor of Nutrition, King's College (KQC), Campden Hill Road, London

Appendix C: Control of Claims Relating to the Presence or Absence of Sugars in Foods

1. Various claims about the nutritional value of foods are controlled by the Food Labelling Regulations 1984,[233] which were made under the Food and Drugs Act 1955 (now the Food Act 1984). The general provisions of the Act itself prohibit the use of any label or advertisement which falsely describes food or misleads as to its nature, substance or quality, including its nutritional or dietary value.

2. Food Labelling Regulations 1984[233] then lay down more specific controls over, for example, claims that a food is an aid to slimming, has a reduced energy value, or is suitable for diabetics. Some of these controls implement the European Community Council Directive relating to the labelling, presentation and advertising of foodstuffs.

3. More recently, claims have been made that certain foods are low, high, reduced, higher in or free from certain nutrients eg "low sugar", "free from added sugar", and there is evidence that these claims are not always soundly based. The Food Advisory Committee considered this issue and has recommended that before certain claims for sugars, fats, fibre and salt are made, either expressly or by implication, certain conditions should be met. For sugars these are as follows:

Claim	Conditions
A reduced sugar(s) content	Total sugars per 100g (or 100ml) must not be more than three quarters of that of a similar food for which no such claim is made.
Low in sugar(s)	Total sugars must not exceed 5g per 100g (or 100ml) *and* total sugars in a normal serving must not exceed 5g.
Sugar(s) – free	Total sugars must not exceed 0.1g per 100g (or per 100ml).
No added sugar/ unsweetened	No mono- or di-saccharides or foods composed mainly of these sugars should have been added to the food or any of its ingredients.

4. The Committee also recommended that when any of these claims were made on a label or in an advertisement, the food should carry full nutritional labelling, showing per 100g (or 100ml) its energy, protein, carbohydrate, total sugars, fat, saturated fatty acids, sodium and fibre contents.

5. These recommendations have been issued by the Ministry of Agriculture, Fisheries and Food for consultation with interested parties.

Appendix D: Evaluation of the Main Dietary Carbohydrates

The following energy yields have been found experimentally for the main carbohydrates in food when burned in a calorimeter.[234]

	Per gram		Per gram of monosaccharide equivalent	
	kcal	kJ	kcal	kJ
Glucose	3.72	15.6	3.72	15.6
Sucrose	3.94	16.5	3.74	15.7
Starch	4.18	17.5	3.76	15.7

The yields per gram differ because of the different proportions of carbon, hydrogen and oxygen in monosaccharides, disaccharides and polysaccharides but when each is converted to its monosaccharide equivalent (the form in which it is absorbed) the energy yields are essentially identical. This is the basis for the UK practice for expressing the energy value of carbohydrate-containing foods in food composition tables and for food labelling.[12, 233]

Before 1978, intakes in the UK shown in tables 3 to 6 were calculated from unpublished tables of nutrient composition compiled in 1968 by the Ministry of Health. They were based on the third edition (1960) of McCance and Widdowson's 'The Composition of Foods'[235] with additional recipes and manufacturer's information. These provided values for total carbohydrate and for extrinsic sugars (defined in para 2.15.2) which were expressed as monosaccharide units. After 1978, nutrient intakes were calculated from the fourth edition of McCance and Widdowson's 'The Composition of Foods'[12] with some additional recipe data[236] and manufacturer's information. These provided values for total carbohydrate and total sugars including the concentrations of sucrose, lactose, glucose, fructose and maltose. The estimates of total energy intake in the fourth edition are on average 3.5 per cent lower, and of carbohydrate intakes 6.0 per cent lower, than those in the third edition.[237] Some of the studies in this Report have included values for non-milk extrinsic ('added') sugars (recipe sugars plus table sugars as defined in para 2.17) in the database derived from the fourth edition[12] and have calculated intakes of both total sugars and non-milk extrinsic ('added') sugars.[24, 25, 32, 33, 34, 211, 212, 216, 217, 221, 227, 230]

Appendix E: Nutrient Intakes and Sugars Consumption

The full data calculated for tables 9 to 12 are presented in the appendices to each table on pages 92–101.

Appendix to Table 9: *Nutrient intake of 105 men and 112 women in Cambridge according to thirds of the distribution of energy intake*

	Men				Women			
	Lower	Middle	Upper	t	Lower	Middle	Upper	t
Total intake (per day)								
Number	35	35	35	(df=68)	37	38	37	(df=72)
Energy, kcal	2168	2673	3448	12.6+++	1475	1944	2416	15.5+++
Range	1443–2418	2427–2953	3003–5024		794–1775	1791–2134	2150–3318	
Nutrient intake								
Potassium mg	3167	3652	4216	4.6+++	2224	2867	3254	9.0+++
Calcium mg	832	1147	1350	7.1+++	667	934	1080	6.8+++
Magnesium mg	266	321	392	5.2+++	188	241	292	8.7+++
Phosphorus mg	1192	1473	1786	9.2+++	911	1166	1346	7.2+++
Iron mg	11.1	13.1	16.4	8.4+++	8.5	9.9	12.2	5.5+++
Copper mg	1.65	1.73	2.41	3.5+++	1.23	1.41	1.53	2.6+
Zinc mg	9.2	10.8	13.2	7.3+++	6.9	8.0	9.5	5.5+++
Chloride mg	4017	5303	6914	10.0+++	3039	3577	4431	6.4+++
Thiamin mg	1.11	1.30	1.53	5.6+++	0.78	1.04	1.14	6.2+++
Riboflavin mg	1.74	2.17	2.61	5.2+++	1.52	1.81	1.92	2.7++
Nicotinic acid mg	16.6	18.6	22.8	4.7+++	11.8	13.5	15.4	4.0+++
Tryptophan/60 mg	15.6	18.1	22.8	8.8+++	11.4	13.9	15.9	7.3+++
Vitamin B6 mg	1.20	1.33	1.64	4.9+++	0.82	1.05	1.14	7.1+++
Folic acid µg	155	194	233	5.0+++	120	139	171	3.9+++
Vitamin B12 µg	7.28	7.18	12.36	2.4+	6.86	6.01	5.77	0.8ns
Vitamin C mg	48	59	63	2.9++	42	51	69	3.0++
Vitamin E mg	4.31	5.44	6.73	7.0+++	3.41	4.21	5.37	6.1+++
Vitamin D µg	2.33	2.83	4.36	3.7+++	2.22	2.12	2.82	1.4ns
Retinol µg	1453	1204	2220	1.5ns	1406	1212	1145	0.8ns
Carotene µg	2667	3286	2481	0.3ns	2125	2225	2774	1.4ns

Appendix to Table 9: (Continued)

	Men				Women			
	Lower	Middle	Upper	t	Lower	Middle	Upper	t
Total intake (per day)								
Number	35	35	35	(df=68)	37	38	37	(df=72)
Energy, kcal	2168	2673	3448	12.6+++	1475	1944	2416	15.5+++
Range	1443–2418	2427–2953	3003–5024		794–1775	1791–2134	2150–3318	
Intake/1000 kcal								
Potassium mg	1461	1366	1223	4.5+++	1508	1474	1347	2.9++
Calcium mg	284	429	392	0.4ns	452	480	447	0.1ns
Magnesium mg	123	120	114	1.6ns	127	124	121	0.9ns
Phosphorus mg	550	551	518	1.5ns	618	600	557	2.1+
Iron mg	5.12	4.90	4.77	1.2ns	5.75	5.09	5.05	1.9ns
Copper mg	0.76	0.65	0.70	1.1ns	0.83	0.73	0.63	2.7++
Zinc mg	4.25	4.04	3.83	2.3+	4.67	4.12	3.92	3.0++
Chloride mg	1853	1984	2005	1.9ns	2060	1891	1834	1.8ns
Thiamin mg	0.51	0.49	0.44	2.0+	0.53	0.53	0.47	1.8ns
Riboflavin mg	0.80	0.81	0.76	0.7ns	1.03	0.93	0.79	2.7++
Nicotinic acid mg	7.7	6.9	6.6	2.4+	8.0	6.9	6.4	3.3++
Tryptophan/60 mg	7.2	6.8	6.6	2.8++	7.8	7.1	6.6	3.9+++
Vitamin B6 mg	0.55	0.50	0.47	2.9++	0.56	0.54	0.47	3.5+++
Folic acid μg	71	72	67	0.9ns	81	72	71	1.3ns
Vitamin B12 μg	3.35	2.69	3.58	0.3ns	4.65	3.09	2.39	2.8++
Vitamin C mg	22	22	18	1.7ns	28	26	29	0.1ns
Vitamin E mg	1.99	2.04	1.95	0.0ns	2.31	2.17	2.22	0.3ns
Vitamin D μg	1.08	1.06	1.26	1.1ns	1.50	1.09	1.17	1.2ns
Retinol μg	670	450	644	0.0ns	993	623	474	2.5+
Carotene μg	1230	1229	720	2.5+	1441	1144	1148	0.9ns

+++ p<0.001; ++ p<0.01; + p<0.05; ns = not significant (lower *vs* upper)
Data of Nelson and Paul (unpublished)

Appendix to Table 10: Nutrient intake of 105 men and 112 women in Cambridge according to the proportion of sugar in the diet (expressed as grams of extrinsic sugar per 1000 kcal)

	Men				Women			
	Lower	Middle	Upper	t	Lower	Middle	Upper	t
Number	35	35	35	(df=68)	37	38	37	(df=72)
Extrinsic sugars g per 1000 kcal	20.4	38.6	55.4	13.0+++	15.6	28.8	49.6	14.5+++
Range	9.0–30.6	31.2–43.1	43.9–109.6		5.2–22.3	22.4–36.5	36.9–111.2	
Nutrient intake								
Potassium mg	3571	3951	3514	0.3ns	2685	2915	2744	0.3ns
Calcium mg	1122	1185	1023	1.1ns	906	937	837	0.8ns
Magnesium mg	324	367	287	2.2+	241	251	228	0.8ns
Phosphorus mg	1499	1592	1359	1.7ns	1171	1197	1054	1.5ns
Iron mg	14.0	14.1	12.5	1.7ns	10.6	10.8	9.2	2.0+
Copper mg	1.86	2.10	1.83	0.1ns	1.39	1.50	1.28	0.9ns
Zinc mg	11.3	11.8	10.2	1.8ns	8.5	8.4	7.4	2.0+
Chloride mg	5298	5974	4961	0.9ns	3874	3768	3504	1.3ns
Thiamin mg	1.32	1.40	1.22	1.1ns	0.98	1.05	0.92	0.8ns
Riboflavin mg	2.11	2.25	2.15	0.2ns	1.80	1.82	1.63	1.0ns
Nicotinic acid mg	19.5	20.6	17.8	1.3ns	13.8	14.3	12.6	1.3ns
Tryptophan/60 mg	18.9	20.3	17.2	1.8ns	14.1	14.4	12.7	1.8ns
Vitamin B6 mg	1.34	1.51	1.31	0.4ns	0.99	1.05	0.98	0.1ns
Folic acid µg	193	220	169	1.6ns	158	150	122	2.6++
Vitamin B12 µg	8.52	8.83	9.46	0.4ns	7.46	6.36	4.81	2.1++
Vitamin C mg	55	62	53	0.4ns	54	53	54	0.0ns
Vitamin E mg	5.78	5.83	4.86	2.2+	4.50	4.41	4.07	1.1ns
Vitamin D µg	3.58	0.22	2.72	1.5ns	2.52	2.27	2.36	0.3ns
Retinol µg	1578	1421	1878	0.6ns	1568	1249	944	2.0+
Carotene µg	3339	2944	2151	2.6++	2641	2743	1725	2.4+

Appendix to Table 10: (Continued)

	Men				Women			
	Lower	Middle	Upper	t	Lower	Middle	Upper	t
Number	35	35	35	(df=68)	37	38	37	(df=72)
Extrinsic sugars g per 1000 kcal	20.4	38.6	55.4	13.0	15.6	28.8	49.6	14.5+++
Range	9.0–30.6	31.2–43.1	43.9–109.6		5.2–22.3	22.4–36.5	36.9–111.2	
Intake/1000 kcal								
Potassium mg	1376	1310	1312	1.0ns	1471	1441	1382	1.3ns
Calcium mg	433	393	382	1.5ns	496	463	422	2.3+
Magnesium mg	125	122	107	4.0+++	132	124	115	2.3+
Phosphorus mg	578	528	507	3.8+++	642	591	530	3.7+++
Iron mg	5.38	4.68	4.68	3.4++	5.82	5.33	4.61	4.1+++
Copper mg	0.72	0.70	0.68	0.8ns	0.76	0.74	0.64	1.1ns
Zinc mg	4.36	3.91	3.80	3.8+++	4.66	4.17	3.74	3.8+++
Chloride mg	2042	1981	1852	2.6+	2122	1862	1765	3.6+++
Thiamin mg	0.51	0.46	0.46	2.0+	0.54	0.51	0.46	2.4+
Riboflavin mg	0.81	0.75	0.80	0.0ns	0.99	0.89	0.82	1.7ns
Nicotinic acid mg	7.5	6.8	6.7	2.2+	7.5	7.1	6.3	2.5+
Tryptophan/60 mg	7.3	6.7	6.4	4.8+++	7.8	7.1	6.4	4.7+++
Vitamin B6 mg	0.52	0.50	0.49	1.3ns	0.54	0.52	0.49	1.7ns
Folic acid µg	74	73	63	2.7++	87	74	62	3.0++
Vitamin B12 µg	3.28	2.92	3.53	0.2ns	4.08	3.14	2.42	1.5ns
Vitamin C mg	21	20	20	1.0ns	30	26	27	0.6ns
Vitamin E mg	2.22	1.93	1.81	3.1++	2.46	2.18	2.05	2.9++
Vitamin D µg	1.38	1.07	1.01	1.7ns	1.38	1.12	1.19	0.9ns
Retinol µg	608	471	701	1.3ns	859	617	476	1.7ns
Carotene µg	1287	976	803	2.7++	1447	1356	869	2.6+

+++$p<0.001$; ++<0.01; +$p0.05$; ns = not significant (lower *vs* upper)
Data of Nelson and Paul (unpublished)

Appendix to Table 11: *Nutrient intake according to intake of non-milk extrinsic sugars within three levels of energy intake in Cambridge adults*

CAMBRIDGE MEN (n=105)

	Highest (3003–5042)			Middle (2427–2953)			Lowest (1443–2418)		
Energy intake (kcal)	Higher	p	Lower	Higher	p	Lower	Higher	p	Lower
Non-milk extrinsic sugars intake (g per 1000 kcal)	41.1–99.4		19.0–41.0	41.5–109.6		9.0–41.3	32.8–84.1		9.6–32.0
number	18		17	18		17	18		17
Nutrient intake									
Potassium mg	4381	0.8ns	4042	3687	0.3ns	3614	3027	1.3ns	3316
Calcium mg	1388	0.6ns	1309	1154	0.1ns	1139	820	0.2ns	845
Magnesium mg	401	0.3ns	383	307	1.6ns	335	261	0.4ns	270
Phosphorus mg	1795	0.1ns	1776	1452	0.5ns	1495	1159	0.8ns	1226
Iron mg	16.5	0.1ns	16.4	12.1	2.1+	14.1	10.77	0.7ns	11.5
Copper mg	2.56	0.8ns	2.24	1.72	0.1ns	1.75	1.58	0.6ns	1.73
Zinc mg	12.9	0.7ns	13.6	10.3	1.4ns	11.3	8.66	1.8ns	9.8
Chloride mg	7017	0.4ns	6804	5106	1.3ns	5512	3947	0.5ns	4091
Thiamin mg	1.50	0.5ns	1.56	1.30	0.0ns	1.30	1.02	1.9ns	1.20
Riboflavin mg	2.67	0.5ns	2.55	2.23	0.5ns	2.11	1.74	0.0ns	1.73
Nicotinic acid mg	22.6	0.1ns	23.0	17.7	1.4ns	19.5	15.8	1.1ns	17.5
Tryptophan/60 mg	22.7	0.1ns	22.9	17.6	1.3ns	18.6	14.8	1.9ns	16.4
Vitamin B6 mg	1.64	0.0ns	1.64	1.33	0.0ns	1.33	1.15	0.9ns	1.25
Folic acid µg	238	0.3ns	229	183	1.2ns	205	147	1.3ns	164
Vitamin B12 µg	13.18	0.5ns	11.48	8.24	0.9ns	6.06	6.34	0.7ns	8.27
Vitamin C mg	66	0.8ns	59	61	0.3ns	58	42	1.6ns	53
Vitamin E mg	6.46	1.0ns	7.82	4.90	2.5+	6.00	4.22	0.4ns	4.40
Vitamin D µg	4.29	0.1ns	4.43	2.33	2.1+	3.45	2.35	0.1ns	2.31
Retinol µg	2468	0.7ns	1957	1364	0.7ns	1035	1478	0.0ns	1428
Carotene µg	2718	0.8ns	2230	2469	2.3+	4151	1889	2.1+	3490

Appendix to Table 11: (Continued)

	CAMBRIDGE MEN (n=105)								
Energy intake (kcal)	Highest (3003–5042)			Middle (2427–2953)			Lowest (1443–2418)		
Non-milk extrinsic sugars intake (g per 1000 kcal)	Higher 41.1–99.4	p	Lower 19.0–41.0	Higher 41.5–109.6	p	Lower 9.0–41.3	Higher 32.8–84.1	p	Lower 9.6–32.0
number	18		17	18		17	18		17
Intake/1000 kcal									
Potassium mg	1191	0.7ns	1240	1376	0.2ns	1361	1382	1.9ns	1539
Calcium mg	384	0.6ns	402	429	0.0ns	428	383	0.0ns	386
Magnesium mg	109	1.0ns	118	115	1.9ns	126	119	0.9ns	126
Phosphorus mg	496	2.4+	546	540	0.8ns	562	532	1.1ns	566
Iron mg	4.65	1.3ns	5.02	4.50	2.4+	5.31	4.87	1.4ns	5.33
Copper mg	0.68	0.1ns	0.69	0.64	0.3ns	0.66	0.71	0.9ns	0.80
Zinc mg	3.58	3.0++	4.16	3.83	1.8ns	4.27	3.95	2.6+	4.56
Chloride mg	1936	1.4ns	2086	1893	1.6ns	2080	1819	0.7ns	1902
Thiamin mg	0.42	1.5ns	0.48	0.48	0.2ns	0.49	0.47	2.0+	0.56
Riboflavin mg	0.73	1.0ns	0.79	0.83	0.4ns	0.80	0.80	0.0ns	0.80
Nicotinic acid mg	6.2	1.8ns	7.1	6.6	1.6ns	7.4	7.21	1.1ns	8.14
Tryptophan/60 mg	6.2	4.1+++	7.0	6.6	1.7ns	7.0	6.8	2.9++	7.6
Vitamin B6 mg	0.45	1.9ns	0.50	0.50	0.1ns	0.50	0.52	1.4ns	0.58
Folic acid µg	65	1.0ns	71	68	1.4ns	77	67	1.6ns	76
Vitamin B12 µg	3.56	0.0ns	3.53	3.05	0.9ns	2.30	2.86	0.8ns	3.79
Vitamin C mg	19	0.1ns	18	23	0.2ns	22	19	1.7ns	25
Vitamin E mg	1.85	1.7ns	2.16	1.82	2.6+	2.26	1.95	0.4ns	2.04
Vitamin D µg	1.24	0.3ns	1.34	0.86	2.2+	1.26	1.10	0.1ns	1.08
Retinol µg	683	0.4ns	603	502	0.6ns	390	659	0.0ns	645
Carotene µg	762	0.5ns	686	916	2.4+	1554	853	2.1+	1592

+++p<0.001; ++p<0.01; +p<0.05; ns = not significant
Data of Nelson and Paul (unpublished)

Appendix to Table 11: *(continued)*

	CAMBRIDGE WOMEN (n=112)								
Energy intake (kcal)	Highest (2150-3318)			Middle (1791-2134)			Lowest (794-1777)		
Non-milk extrinsic sugars intake (g per 1000 kcal)	Higher	p	Lower	Higher	p	Lower	Higher	p	Lower
	32.8-84.4		10.9-31.8	26.2-71.0		12.0-25.9	23.8-111.1		5.2-19.9
Number	18		19	19		19	18		19
Nutrient intake									
Potassium mg	3246	0.0ns	3261	2962	1.4ns	2773	2085	1.7ns	2355
Calcium mg	1080	0.0ns	1079	881	1.2ns	986	591	1.8ns	740
Magnesium mg	289	0.4ns	297	241	0.0ns	241	166	2.4+	208
Phosphorus mg	1310	0.8ns	1381	1122	1.2ns	1210	814	2.3+	1003
Iron mg	11.6	1.4ns	12.9	9.2	2.4ns	10.6	7.4	2.1+	9.5
Copper mg	1.51	0.3ns	1.56	1.28	1.5ns	1.54	1.22	0.0ns	1.23
Zinc mg	9.0	1.7ns	10.0	7.7	1.5ns	8.3	6.2	2.2+	7.6
Chloride mg	4414	0.1ns	4451	3564	1.6ns	3791	2676	2.1+	3383
Thiamin mg	1.10	1.1ns	1.18	1.05	0.4ns	1.02	0.74	0.9ns	0.83
Riboflavin mg	1.93	0.1ns	1.91	1.73	0.9ns	1.89	1.44	0.7ns	1.60
Nicotinic acid mg	14.8	1.1ns	16.0	13.4	0.2ns	13.6	10.90	1.2ns	12.6
Tryptophan/60 mg	15.5	1.2ns	16.4	13.3	1.7ns	14.4	10.3	2.4+	12.5
Vitamin B6 mg	1.13	0.3ns	1.15	1.04	0.2ns	1.06	0.78	1.1.ns	0.86
Folic acid µg	152	3.0++	193	133	1.0ns	145	104	1.5ns	136
Vitamin B12 µg	4.85	1.2ns	6.65	4.36	1.9ns	7.65	6.59	0.2ns	7.11
Vitamin C mg	74	0.6ns	64	45	1.6ns	56	37	1.0ns	46
Vitamin E mg	5.28	0.3ns	5.45	3.87	2.1+	4.55	3.02	1.9ns	3.78
Vitamin D µg	2.82	0.0ns	2.82	1.91	1.5ns	2.33	1.93	0.7ns	2.89
Retinol µg	1118	0.1ns	1173	679	2.7+	1745	1297	0.3ns	1509
Carotene µg	1842	2.9++	3657	2118	0.0ns	2333	2023	0.3ns	2221

Appendix to Table 11: (Continued)

	CAMBRIDGE WOMEN (n=112)								
Energy intake (kcal)	Highest (2150–3318)			Middle (1791–2134)			Lowest (794–1777)		
	Higher		Lower	Higher		Lower	Higher		Lower
Non-milk extrinsic sugars intake (g per 1000 kcal)	32.8–84.4	p	10.9–31.8	26.2–71.0	p	12.0–25.9	23.8–111.1	p	5.2–19.9
Number	18		19	19		19	18		19
Intake/1000 kcal									
Potassium mg	1304	1.3ns	1407	1534	1.6ns	1423	1470	1.1ns	1567
Calcium mg	403	0.8ns	466	455	1.2ns	504	412	1.8ns	488
Magnesium mg	116	1.9ns	129	125	0.0ns	124	116	2.7+	137
Phosphorus mg	525	2.0ns	593	597	1.2ns	620	571	2.3+	663
Iron mg	4.63	3.2++	5.56	4.78	2.2+	5.41	5.20	1.6ns	6.21
Copper mg	0.60	1.4ns	0.67	0.66	1.4ns	0.79	0.92	0.7ns	0.80
Zinc mg	3.62	3.3++	4.34	3.96	1.3ns	4.27	4.34	1.6ns	5.03
Chloride mg	1769	1.4ns	1924	1841	1.5ns	1944	1859	2.0+	2199
Thiamin mg	0.44	2.2+	0.51	0.55	0.7ns	0.52	0.52	0.5ns	0.55
Riboflavin mg	0.77	0.6ns	0.82	0.89	0.8ns	0.97	1.04	0.1ns	1.06
Nicotinic acid mg	5.9	2.1+	6.9	6.9	0.0ns	7.0	7.78	0.6ns	8.37
Tryptophan/60 mg	6.2	2.7++	7.0	6.9	1.6ns	7.4	7.2	2.4+	8.3
Vitamin B6 mg	0.45	1.6ns	0.50	0.54	0.0ns	0.54	0.55	0.6ns	0.57
Folic acid μg	61	3.9++	83	69	0.9ns	75	73	1.0ns	89
Vitamin B12 μg	4.05	1.5ns	2.78	2.28	1.8ns	3.97	5.21	0.4ns	4.47
Vitamin C mg	30	0.3ns	28	23	1.6ns	29	26	0.8ns	30
Vitamin E mg	2.12	1.1ns	2.34	2.00	2.0+	2.33	2.08	1.9ns	2.46
Vitamin D μg	1.13	0.3ns	1.19	0.99	1.5ns	1.19	1.26	0.5ns	1.61
Retinol μg	429	0.4ns	486	354	2.6+	903	1037	0.2ns	948
Carotene μg	750	3.0++	1598	1081	0.5ns	1205	1373	0.2ns	1462

+++p<0.001; ++p<0.01; +p<0.05; ns = not significant
Data of Nelson and Paul (unpublished)

Appendix to Table 12: Nutrient intake of 195 women in the first trimester of pregnancy in Leeds according to intake of extrinsic sugars within three levels of energy intake

Energy intake	Highest			Middle			Lowest		
Non-milk extrinsic sugars intake (g per 1000 kcal)	Higher 43.4	p	Lower 23.2	Higher 43.1	p	Lower 24.0	Higher 42.4	p	Lower 18.0
Nutrient intake									
Potassium mg	3088	1.3ns	3267	2485	2.8++	2766	1834	1.5ns	2025
Calcium mg	1115	0.5ns	1150	902	0.5ns	930	619	0.6ns	653
Magnesium mg	258	0.6ns	265	212	0.6ns	219	153	0.7ns	159
Phosphorus mg	1353	1.2ns	1429	1116	1.0ns	1170	797	2.1+	900
Iron mg	10.7	1.6ns	11.5	9.2	0.1ns	9.3	6.5	3.1++	7.7
Copper mg	1.64	1.1ns	1.81	1.34	0.4ns	1.30	1.00	1.2ns	1.12
Zinc mg	9.4	2.0+	10.4	7.9	0.9ns	8.3	5.6	3.4++	7.0
Chloride mg	4443	1.8ns	4828	3711	2.0+	4044	2788	1.7ns	3052
Thiamin mg	1.22	1.6ns	1.32	0.99	1.6ns	1.08	0.75	2.0+	0.85
Riboflavin mg	2.07	0.3ns	2.12	1.73	0.3ns	1.68	1.14	2.3+	1.39
Nicotinic acid mg	14.6	1.1ns	15.7	12.7	0.0ns	12.8	9.1	3.3++	11.4
Tryptophan/60 mg	16.5	2.6+	18.2	13.5	2.7++	15.0	10.2	3.2++	12.3
Vitamin B6 mg	1.26	1.9ns	1.38	1.05	1.6ns	1.13	0.79	2.3+	0.92
Folic acid µg	173	1.6ns	191	144	0.5ns	148	111	1.2ns	123
Vitamin B12 µg	7.20	0.7ns	8.15	6.34	1.3ns	5.09	4.73	1.5ns	6.43
Vitamin C mg	78	0.1ns	76	58	0.2ns	60	41	0.0ns	41
Vitamin E mg	4.70	1.9ns	5.23	3.88	1.5ns	4.20	2.82	1.3ns	3.14
Vitamin D µg	3.10	0.5ns	2.90	2.18	0.0ns	2.18	1.77	0.8ns	2.02
Retinol µg	1178	1.1ns	1502	1020	1.5ns	680	715	1.2ns	1020
Carotene µg	1903	1.4ns	2517	1785	0.8ns	1545	935	0.5ns	1054

Appendix to Table 12: *Nutrient intake of 195 women in the first trimester of pregnancy in Leeds according to intake of extrinsic sugars within three levels of energy intake*

Energy intake	Highest			Middle			Lowest		
Non-milk extrinsic sugars intake (g per 1000 kcal)	Higher 43.4	p	Lower 23.2	Higher 43.1	p	Lower 24.0	Higher 42.4	p	Lower 18.0
Intake/1000 kcal									
Potassium mg	1334	1.1ns	1384	1321	2.4+	1450	1280	2.8++	1455
Calcium mg	485	0.0ns	485	480	0.2ns	487	436	1.0ns	467
Magnesium mg	111	0.0ns	112	113	0.3ns	115	107	2.2+	115
Phosphorus mg	587	0.7ns	605	593	0.7ns	612	562	3.3++	652
Iron mg	4.64	1.3ns	4.91	4.87	0.1ns	4.83	4.57	4.1+++	5.62
Copper mg	0.71	0.9ns	0.77	0.71	0.6ns	0.68	0.71	1.6ns	0.82
Zinc mg	4.07	1.7ns	4.42	4.20	0.6ns	4.34	3.95	3.9+++	5.10
Chloride mg	1933	1.3ns	2041	1969	1.9ns	2114	1970	2.4+	2238
Thiamin mg	0.53	1.2ns	0.56	0.52	1.7ns	0.57	0.53	2.8++	0.61
Riboflavin mg	0.90	0.0ns	0.90	0.92	0.5ns	0.88	0.81	2.9++	1.01
Nicotinic acid mg	6.3	0.9ns	6.7	6.7	0.0ns	6.7	6.4	4.1+++	8.3
Tryptophan/60 mg	7.2	2.1+	7.7	7.2	2.4+	7.8	7.2	4.1+++	8.3
Vitamin B6 mg	0.55	1.7ns	0.58	0.56	1.3ns	0.59	0.55	3.6+++	0.67
Folic acid µg	75	1.3ns	81	76	0.3ns	77	78	1.0ns	89
Vitamin B12 µg	3.09	0.7ns	3.49	3.38	1.4ns	2.65	3.34	1.7ns	4.67
Vitamin C mg	34	0.4ns	32	31	0.1ns	32	29	0.1ns	29
Vitamin E mg	2.03	1.7ns	2.21	2.06	1.2ns	2.2	2.01	1.5ns	2.29
Vitamin D µg	1.32	0.5ns	1.23	1.15	0.1ns	1.14	1.25	1.1ns	1.56
Retinol µg	504	1.0ns	637	544	1.6ns	354	508	1.3ns	741
Carotene µg	829	1.3ns	1070	939	1.0ns	799	638	0.9ns	758

+++p<0.00; ++p<0.01; +p<0.05; ns = not significant

Data of Smithells *et al*[30] and unpublished

Printed in the United Kingdom for HMSO.
Dd.0293083, 3/91, C8, 3385/4, 5673, 141696.